INTERNATIONAL TERRORISM

CONVENTIONS, RESOLUTIONS, LEGISLATIONS, TERRORIST ORGANISATIONS AND TERRORISTS

VOLUME I

Edited by

K.R. GUPTA

ATLANTIC

ATLANTIC PUBLISHERS AND DISTRIBUTORS

Published by
ATLANTIC PUBLISHERS AND DISTRIBUTORS
B-2, Vishal Enclave, Opp. Rajouri Garden, New Delhi-27
Phones : 5413460, 5429987

Sales Office
4215/1, Ansari Road, Darya Ganj, New Delhi-02
Phones : 3273880, 3285873, 3280451
Fax : 91-11-3285873
e-mail : info@atlanticbooks.com
web : www.atlanticbooks.com

ISBN 81-269-0107-1 (Vol. I)
ISBN 81-269-0108-X (Vol. II)
ISBN 81-269-0109-8 (Set)

Typeset at
APD Computer Graphics, Delhi

Printed in India at
Mehra Offset Press, Delhi

PREFACE

Terrorism now has become a world-wide phenomenon. During the last two decades the world has been marked by an increasing number of terrorist attacks. Terrorism occurs when a group, whether holding governmental office, or outside government, resolves to pursue a set of ideological objectives by methods which not only subvert or ignore the requirements of domestic and international law, but which rely for their success primarily upon the threat or use of violence. There are now over one lakh *jehadis* all over the Islamic world, in Afghanistan, Kashmir, Albania, Chechnaya (Russia), Xin-jiang (China), Central Asia and elsewhere.

Over the years, the United Nations, the regional organisations and different individual countries have formulated a number of laws and conventions, passed resolutions, and framed legislations to combat terrorism. An attempt has been made in this book to bring these laws, conventions, resolutions and legislations at one place.

It is hoped that the book would be found useful by the executives of the world and regional organisations, non-government organisations concerned with world peace and security, government executives and parliamentarians in different countries concerned with tackling terrorism, students of political science and the common man interested in day-to-day world affairs.

K.R. GUPTA

CONTENTS

VOLUME II

—Ali Saed Bin Ali El-Hoorie
—Anas Al-Liby
—Ayman Al-Zawahiri
—Fazul Abdullah Mohammed
—Hasan Izz-Al-Din
—Ibrahim Salih Mohammed Al-Yacoub
—Imad Fayez Mugniyah
—Khalid Shaikh Mohammed
—Muhammad Atef
—Muhsin Musa Matwalli Atwah
—Mustafa Mohamed Fadhil
—Saif Al-Adel
—Usama Bin Laden

1

Resolution 1373 (2001) Adopted by the Security Council at its 4385th meeting on 28 September 2001

The Security Council,

Reaffirming its resolutions 1269 (1999) of 19 October 1999 and 1368 (2001) of 12 September 2001,

Reaffirming also its unequivocal condemnation of the terrorist attacks which took place in New York, Washington, D.C. and Pennsylvania on 11 September 2001, and expressing its determination to prevent all such acts,

Reaffirming further that such acts, like any act of international terrorism, constitute a threat to international peace and security,

Reaffirming the inherent right of individual or collective self-defence as recognized by the Charter of the United Nations as reiterated in resolution 1368 (2001),

Reaffirming the need to combat by all means, in accordance with the Charter of the United Nations, threats to international peace and security caused by terrorist acts,

Deeply concerned by the increase, in various regions of the world, of acts of terrorism motivated by intolerance or extremism,

Calling on States to work together urgently to prevent and suppress terrorist acts, including through increased cooperation and full implementation of the relevant international conventions relating to terrorism,

Recognizing the need for States to complement international cooperation by taking additional measures to prevent and suppress, in their territories through all lawful means, the financing and preparation of any acts of terrorism,

Reaffirming the principle established by the General Assembly in its declaration of October 1970 (resolution 2625 (XXV)) and reiterated by the Security Council in its resolution 1189 (1998) of 13 August 1998, namely that every State has the duty to refrain from organizing, instigating, assisting or participating in terrorist acts in another State or acquiescing in organized activities within its territory directed towards the commission of such acts,

Acting under Chapter VII of the Charter of the United Nations,

1. *Decides* that all States shall :

(a) Prevent and suppress the financing of terrorist acts;

(b) Criminalize the wilful provision or collection, by any means, directly or indirectly, of funds by their nationals or in their territories with the intention that the funds should be used, or in the knowledge that they are to be used, in order to carry out terrorist acts;

(c) Freeze without delay funds and other financial assets or economic resources of persons who commit, or attempt to commit, terrorist acts or participate in or facilitate the commission of terrorist acts; of entities owned or controlled directly or indirectly by such persons; and of persons and entities acting on behalf of, or at the direction of such persons and entities, including funds derived or generated from property owned or controlled directly or indirectly by such persons and associated persons and entities;

(d) Prohibit their nationals or any persons and entities within their territories from making any funds, financial assets or economic resources or financial or other related services available, directly or indirectly, for the benefit of persons who commit or attempt to commit or facilitate or participate in the commission of terrorist acts, of entities owned or controlled, directly or indirectly, by such persons and of persons and entities acting on behalf of or at the direction of such persons;

2. *Decides also* that all States shall :

(a) Refrain from providing any form of support, active or passive, to entities or persons involved in terrorist acts, including by suppressing recruitment of members of terrorist groups and eliminating the supply of weapons to terrorists;

(b) Take the necessary steps to prevent the commission of terrorist acts, including by provision of early warning to other States by exchange of information;

(c) Deny safe haven to those who finance, plan, support, or commit terrorist acts, or provide safe havens;

(d) Prevent those who finance, plan, facilitate or commit terrorist acts from using their respective territories for those purposes against other States or their citizens;

(e) Ensure that any person who participates in the financing, planning, preparation or perpetration of terrorist acts or in supporting terrorist acts is brought to justice and ensure that, in addition to any other measures against them, such terrorist acts are established as serious criminal offences in domestic laws and regulations and that the punishment duly reflects the seriousness of such terrorist acts;

(f) Afford one another the greatest measure of assistance in connection with criminal investigations or criminal proceedings relating to the financing or support of terrorist acts, including assistance in obtaining evidence in their possession necessary for the proceedings;

(g) Prevent the movement of terrorists or terrorist groups by effective border controls and controls on issuance of identity papers and travel documents, and through measures for preventing counterfeiting, forgery or fraudulent use of identity papers and travel documents;

3. *Calls* upon all States to :

(a) Find ways of intensifying and accelerating the exchange of operational information, especially regarding actions or movements of terrorist persons or networks; forged or falsified travel documents; traffic in arms, explosives or sensitive materials; use of communications technologies by terrorist groups; and the threat posed by the possession of weapons of mass destruction by terrorist groups;

(b) Exchange information in accordance with international and domestic law and cooperate on administrative and judicial matters to prevent the commission of terrorist acts;

(c) Cooperate, particularly through bilateral and multilateral arrangements and agreements, to prevent and suppress terrorist attacks and take action against perpetrators of such acts;

(d) Become parties as soon as possible to the relevant international conventions and protocols relating to terrorism, including the International Convention for the Suppression of the Financing of Terrorism of 9 December 1999;

(e) Increase cooperation and fully implement the relevant international conventions and protocols relating to terrorism and Security Council resolutions 1269 (1999) and 1368 (2001);

(f) Take appropriate measures in conformity with the relevant provisions of national and international law, including international standards of human rights, before granting refugee status, for the purpose of ensuring that the asylum-seeker has not planned, facilitated or participated in the commission of terrorist acts;

(g) Ensure, in conformity with international law, that refugee status is not abused by the perpetrators, organizers or facilitators of terrorist acts, and that claims of political motivation are not recognized as grounds for refusing requests for the extradition of alleged terrorists;

4. *Notes* with concern the close connection between international terrorism and transnational organized crime, illicit drugs, money-laundering, illegal arms-trafficking, and illegal movement of nuclear, chemical, biological and other potentially deadly materials, and in this regard *emphasizes* the need to enhance coordination of efforts on national, subregional, regional and international levels in order to strengthen a global response to this serious challenge and threat to international security;

5. *Declares* that acts, methods, and practices of terrorism are contrary to the purposes and principles of the United Nations and that knowingly financing, planning and inciting terrorist acts are also contrary to the purposes and principles of the United Nations;

6. *Decides* to establish, in accordance with rule 28 of its provisional rules of procedure, a Committee of the Security Council, consisting of all the members of the Council, to monitor implementation of this resolution, with the assistance of appropriate expertise, and *calls upon* all States to report to the Committee, no later than 90 days from the date of adoption of this resolution and thereafter according to a timetable to be proposed by the Committee, on the steps they have taken to implement this resolution;

7. *Directs* the Committee to delineate its tasks, submit a work programme within 30 days of the adoption of this resolution, and to consider the support it requires, in consultation with the Secretary-General;

8. *Expresses* its determination to take all necessary steps in

order to ensure the full implementation of this resolution, in accordance with its responsibilities under the Charter;

9. *Decides* to remain seized of this matter.

2

UN Security Council Anti-Terrorism Resolution (28 September 2001)

Unanimous call for suppressing financing, improving international cooperation

Security Council SC/7158

4385th Meeting (Night)

28 September 2001

Security Council Unanimously Adopts Wide-ranging Anti-terrorism Resolution; Calls For Suppressing Financing, Improving International Cooperation. Resolution 1373 (2001) Also Creates Committee to Monitor Implementation

Reaffirming its unequivocal condemnation of the terrorist acts that took place in New York, Washington, D.C., and Pennsylvania on 11 September, the Security Council this evening unanimously adopted a wide-ranging, comprehensive resolution with steps and strategies to combat international terrorism.

By resolution 1373 (2001) the Council also established a Committee of the Council to monitor the resolution's implementation and called on all States to report on actions they had taken to that end no later than 90 days from today.

Under terms of the text, the Council decided that all States should prevent and suppress the financing of terrorism, as well as criminalize the wilful provision or collection of funds for such acts. The funds, financial assets and economic resources of those who commit or attempt to commit terrorist acts or participate in or facilitate the commission of terrorist acts and of persons and entities acting on behalf of terrorists should also be frozen without delay.

The Council also decided that States should prohibit their nationals or persons or entities in their territories from making funds, financial assets, economic resources, financial or other related services available to persons who commit or attempt to commit, facilitate or participate in the commission of terrorist acts. States should also refrain from providing any form of support to entities or persons involved in terrorist acts; take the necessary steps to prevent the commission of terrorist acts; deny safe haven to those who finance, plan, support, commit terrorist acts and provide safe havens as well.

By other terms, the Council decided that all States should prevent those who finance, plan, facilitate or commit terrorist acts from using their respective territories for those purposes against other countries and their citizens. States should also ensure that anyone who has participated in the financing, planning, preparation or perpetration of terrorist acts or in supporting terrorist acts is brought to justice. They should also ensure that terrorist acts are established as serious criminal offences in domestic laws and regulations and that the seriousness of such acts is duly reflected in sentences served.

By further terms, the Council decided that States should afford one another the greatest measure of assistance for criminal investigations or criminal proceedings relating to the financing or support of terrorist acts. States should also prevent the movement of terrorists or their groups by effective border controls as well.

Also by the text, the Council called on all States to intensify and accelerate the exchange of information regarding terrorist actions or movements; forged or falsified documents; traffic in arms and sensitive material; use of communications and technologies by terrorist groups; and the threat posed by the possession of weapons of mass destruction.

States were also called on to exchange information and cooperate to prevent and suppress terrorist acts and to take action against the perpetrators of such acts. States should become parties to, and fully implement as soon as possible, the relevant international conventions and protocols to combat terrorism.

By the text, before granting refugee status, all States should take appropriate measures to ensure that the asylum seekers had not planned, facilitated or participated in terrorist acts. Further, States should ensure that refugee status was not abused by the perpetrators, organizers or facilitators of terrorist acts, and that claims of political motivation were not recognized as grounds for refusing requests for the extradition of alleged terrorists.

The Council noted with concern the close connection between international terrorism and transnational organized crime, illicit drugs, money laundering and illegal movement of nuclear, chemical, biological and other deadly materials. In that regard, it emphasized the need to enhance the coordination of national, subregional, regional and international efforts to strengthen a global response to that threat to international security.

Reaffirming the need to combat by all means, in accordance with the Charter, threats to international peace and security caused by terrorist acts, the Council expressed its determination to take all necessary steps to fully implement the current resolution.

The meeting, which began at 10 :50 p m., adjourned at 10:53 p.m.

Resolution

The full text of resolution 1373 (2001) reads as follows :

"The Security Council,

"Reaffirming its resolutions 1269 (1999) of 19 October 1999 and 1368 (2001) of 12 September 2001,

"Reaffirming also its unequivocal condemnation of the terrorist attacks which took place in New York, Washington, D.C., and Pennsylvania on 11 September 2001, and expressing its determination to prevent all such acts,

"Reaffirming further that such acts, like any act of international terrorism, constitute a threat to international peace and security,

"Reaffirming the inherent right of individual or collective self-defence as recognized by the Charter of the United Nations as reiterated in resolution 1368 (2001),

"Reaffirming the need to combat by all means, in accordance with the Charter of the United Nations, threats to international peace and security caused by terrorist acts,

"Deeply concerned by the increase, in various regions of the world, of acts of terrorism motivated by intolerance or extremism,

"Calling on States to work together urgently to prevent and suppress terrorist acts, including through increased cooperation and full implementation of the relevant international conventions relating to terrorism,

"Recognizing the need for States to complement international cooperation by taking additional measures to prevent and suppress, in their territories through all lawful means, the financing and preparation of any acts of terrorism,

"Reaffirming the principle established by the General Assembly in its declaration of October 1970 (resolution 2625 (XXV)) and reiterated by the Security Council in its resolution 1189 (1998) of 13 August 1998, namely that every State has the duty to refrain from organizing, instigating, assisting or participating in terrorist acts in another State or acquiescing in organized activities within its territory directed towards the commission of such acts,

"Acting under Chapter VII of the Charter of the United Nations,

"1. Decides that all States shall :

"(a) Prevent and suppress the financing of terrorist acts;

"(b) Criminalize the wilful provision or collection, by any means, directly or indirectly, of funds by their nationals or in their territories with the intention that the funds should be used, or in the knowledge that they are to be used, in order to carry out terrorist acts;

"(c) Freeze without delay funds and other financial assets or economic resources of persons who commit, or attempt to commit, terrorist acts or participate in or facilitate the commission of terrorist acts; of entities owned or controlled directly or indirectly by such persons; and of persons and entities acting on behalf of, or at the direction of such persons and entities, including funds derived or generated from property owned or controlled directly or indirectly by such persons and associated persons and entities;

"(d) Prohibit their nationals or any persons and entities within their territories from making any funds, financial assets or economic resources or financial or other related services available, directly or indirectly, for the benefit of persons who commit or attempt to commit or facilitate or participate in the commission of terrorist acts, of entities owned or controlled, directly or indirectly, by such persons and of persons and entities acting on behalf of or at the direction of such persons;

"2. Decides also that all States shall :

"(a) Refrain from providing any form of support, active or passive, to entities or persons involved in terrorist acts, including by suppressing recruitment of members of terrorist groups and eliminating the supply of weapons to terrorists;

"(b) Take the necessary steps to prevent the commission

of terrorist acts, including by provision of early warning to other States by exchange of information;

"(c) Deny safe haven to those who finance, plan, support, or commit terrorist acts, or provide safe havens;

"(d) Prevent those who finance, plan, facilitate or commit terrorist acts from using their respective territories for those purposes against other States or their citizens;

"(e) Ensure that any person who participates in the financing, planning, preparation or perpetration of terrorist acts or in supporting terrorist acts is brought to justice and ensure that, in addition to any other measures against them, such terrorist acts are established as serious criminal offences in domestic laws and regulations and that the punishment duly reflects the seriousness of such terrorist acts;

"(f) Afford one another the greatest measure of assistance in connection with criminal investigations or criminal proceedings relating to the financing or support of terrorist acts, including assistance in obtaining evidence in their possession necessary for the proceedings;

"(g) Prevent the movement of terrorists or terrorist groups by effective border controls and controls on issuance of identity papers and travel documents, and through measures for preventing counterfeiting, forgery or fraudulent use of identity papers and travel documents;

"3. Calls upon all States to :

"(a) Find ways of intensifying and accelerating the exchange of operational information, especially regarding actions or movements of terrorist persons or networks; forged or falsified travel documents; traffic in arms, explosives or sensitive materials; use of communications technologies by terrorist groups; and the threat posed by the possession of weapons of mass destruction by terrorist groups;

"(b) Exchange information in accordance with international

and domestic law and cooperate on administrative and judicial matters to prevent the commission of terrorist acts;

"(c) Cooperate, particularly through bilateral and multilateral arrangements and agreements, to prevent and suppress terrorist attacks and take action against perpetrators of such acts;

"(d) Become parties as soon as possible to the relevant international conventions and protocols relating to terrorism, including the International Convention for the Suppression of the Financing of Terrorism of 9 December 1999;

"(e) Increase cooperation and fully implement the relevant international conventions and protocols relating to terrorism and Security Council resolutions 1269 (1999) and 1368 (2001);

"(f) Take appropriate measures in conformity with the relevant provisions of national and international law, including international standards of human rights, before granting refugee status, for the purpose of ensuring that the asylum seeker has not planned, facilitated or participated in the commission of terrorist acts;

"(g) Ensure, in conformity with international law, that refugee status is not abused by the perpetrators, organizers or facilitators of terrorist acts, and that claims of political motivation are not recognized as grounds for refusing requests for the extradition of alleged terrorists;

"4. Notes with concern the close connection between international terrorism and transnational organized crime, illicit drugs, money-laundering, illegal arms-trafficking, and illegal movement of nuclear, chemical, biological and other potentially deadly materials, and in this regard emphasizes the need to enhance coordination of efforts on national, subregional, regional and international levels in order to strengthen a global response to this serious challenge and threat to international security;

"5. Declares that acts, methods, and practices of terrorism are contrary to the purposes and principles of the United Nations and that knowingly financing, planning and inciting terrorist acts are also contrary to the purposes and principles of the United Nations;

"6. Decides to establish, in accordance with rule 28 of its provisional rules of procedure, a Committee of the Security Council, consisting of all the members of the Council, to monitor implementation of this resolution, with the assistance of appropriate expertise, and calls upon all States to report to the Committee, no later than 90 days from the date of adoption of this resolution and thereafter according to a timetable to be proposed by the Committee, on the steps they have taken to implement this resolution;

"7. Directs the Committee to delineate its tasks, submit a work programme within 30 days of the adoption of this resolution, and to consider the support it requires, in consultation with the Secretary-General;

"8. Expresses its determination to take all necessary steps in order to ensure the full implementation of this resolution, in accordance with its responsibilities under the Charter;

"9. Decides to remain seized of this matter."

3

Bush Lifts Sanctions Against India, Pakistan (22 September 2001)

Action to begin immediately

President Bush formally lifted sanctions against India and Pakistan September 22 in a special memorandum to Secretary of State Colin Powell.

The sanctions were imposed in response to the Indian and Pakistani nuclear weapons programs and testing. Powell said on NBC's "Meet the Press" September 23 that lifting these sanctions, which had been under consideration for some time, sends an important signal that "we will stand by our friends who stand by us."

Following is the text of Bush's announcement :

The White House
Office of the Press Secretary
September 22, 2001
Presidential Determination
No. 2001-28
Memorandum For The Secretary of State
Subject : Waiver of Nuclear-Related Sanctions on India and Pakistan

Pursuant to section 9001(b) of the Department of Defense Appropriations Act, 2000 (Public Law 106-79), I hereby determine and certify to the Congress that the application to India and Pakistan of the sanctions and prohibitions contained in subparagraphs (B), (C), and (G) of section 102(b)(2) of the

Arms Export Control Act would not be in the national security interests of the United States. Furthermore, pursuant to section 9001(a) of the Department of Defense Appropriations Act, 2000 (Public Law 106-79), I hereby waive, with respect to India and Pakistan, to the extent not already waived, the application of any sanction contained in section 101 or 102 of the Arms Export Control Act, section 2(b)(4) of the Export Import Bank Act of 1945, and section 620E(e) of the Foreign Assistance Act of 1961, as amended.

You are authorized and directed to transmit this determination and certification to the appropriate committees of the Congress and to arrange for its publication in the Federal Register.

4

Resolution adopted by the General Assembly (18 September 2001)

[*without reference to a Main Committee* (*A/56/L.1*)]

56/1. Condemnation of terrorist attacks in the United States of America

The General Assembly,

Guided by the purposes and principles of the Charter of the United Nations,

1. *Strongly condemns* the heinous acts of terrorism, which have caused enormous loss of human life, destruction and damage in the cities of New York, host city of the United Nations, and Washington, D.C., and in Pennsylvania;

2. *Expresses its condolences and solidarity* with the people and Government of the United States of America in these sad and tragic circumstances;

3. *Urgently calls* for international cooperation to bring to justice the perpetrators, organizers and sponsors of the outrages of 11 September 2001;

4. *Also urgently calls* for international cooperation to prevent and eradicate acts of terrorism, and stresses that those responsible for aiding, supporting or harbouring the perpetrators, organizers and sponsors of such acts will be held accountable.

1st plenary meeting
12 September 2001

5

UN Security Council Condemns Terrorist Attacks on U.S. (12 September 2001)

Council expresses determination to combat terrorism

The United Nations Security Council approved a resolution September 12 condemning the terrorist attacks on the United States, and expressed determination to combat threats to international peace and security caused by terrorists.

The measure was approved unanimously as Security Council members stood in silence, a sharp departure from the traditional voting by a show of hands.

Following is the text of the Security Council resolution :

UNSC Resolution
New York
September 12

The Security Council,

Reaffirming the principles and purposes of the Charter of the United Nations,

Determined to combat by all means threats to international peace and security caused by terrorist acts,

Recognizing the inherent right of individual or collective self-defence in accordance with the Charter,

1. Unequivocally condemns in the strongest terms the

horrifying terrorist attacks which took place on 11 September 2001 in New York, Washington (DC) and Pennsylvania and regards such acts as well as any act of terrorism as criminal and unjustifiable, regardless of their motivation;

2. Expresses its deepest sympathy and condolences to the victims and their families and to the people and government of the United States of America;
3. Calls on all states to work together urgently to bring to justice the perpetrators, organizers and sponsors of these terrorist attacks and stresses that those responsible for aiding, supporting or harboring the perpetrators, organizers and sponsors of these acts will be held accountable;
4. Emphasizes that these acts represent a threat to international peace and security and calls on the international community to redouble their efforts to prevent and suppress terrorist acts by increased cooperation and full implementation of the relevant international anti-terrorist conventions and Security Council resolutions, in particular resolution 1269 (1999);
5. Expresses its readiness to take all necessary steps in accordance with its responsibilities under the Charter of the United Nations to respond to the terrorist attacks of 11 September 2001 and to combat terrorism;
6. Decides to remain seized of the matter.

6

UN General Assembly Condemns Terrorist Attacks in the U.S. (12 September 2001)

Urgently calls for international cooperation

United Nations
September 12, 2001
Adoption of the agenda and organization of work resolution of the General Assembly
Condemnation of terrorist attacks in the United States of America

The General Assembly,

Guided by the purposes and principles of the Charter of the United Nations,

1. Strongly condemns the heinous acts of terrorism which have caused enormous loss of human life, destruction and damage in the cities of New York, host city of the United Nations, Washington, D.C., and Pennsylvania;
2. Expresses its condolences and solidarity with the people and Government of the United States of America in these sad and tragic circumstances;
3. Urgently calls for international cooperation to bring to justice the perpetrators, organizers, and sponsors of the outrages of 11 September 2001;
4. Urgently calls for international cooperation to prevent and eradicate acts of terrorism, and stresses that those

responsible for aiding, supporting, or harbouring the perpetrators, organizers and sponsors of such acts will be held accountable.

7

Resolution 1368 (2001) Adopted by the Security Council at its 4370th meeting on 12 September 2001

The Security Council,

Reaffirming the principles and purposes of the Charter of the United Nations,

Determined to combat by all means threats to international peace and security caused by terrorist acts,

Recognizing the inherent right of individual or collective self-defence in accordance with the Charter,

1. *Unequivocally condemns* in the strongest terms the horrifying terrorist attacks which took place on 11 September 2001 in New York, Washington, D.C. and Pennsylvania and *regards* such acts, like any act of international terrorism, as a threat to international peace and security;
2. *Expresses* its deepest sympathy and condolences to the victims and their families and to the people and Government of the United States of America;
3. *Calls* on all States to work together urgently to bring to justice the perpetrators, organizers and sponsors of these terrorist attacks and *stresses* that those responsible for aiding, supporting or harbouring the perpetrators,

organizers and sponsors of these acts will be held accountable;

4. *Calls also* on the international community to redouble their efforts to prevent and suppress terrorist acts including by increased cooperation and full implementation of the relevant international anti-terrorist conventions and Security Council resolutions, in particular resolution 1269 (1999) of 19 October 1999;
5. *Expresses* its readiness to take all necessary steps to respond to the terrorist attacks of 11 September 2001, and to combat all forms of terrorism, in accordance with its responsibilities under the Charter of the United Nations;
6. *Decides* to remain seized of the matter.

8

CHOGM Summit Excerpts from The Durban Communique (01 May 2001)

Terrorism

33. Heads of Government reaffirmed their strongest condemnation of acts of terrorism in all its forms and manifestations, which destabilise the political, economic and social order of sovereign states. They reiterated their determination to promote international and regional co-operation and to strengthen the international legal framework to ensure that terrorists do not find safe haven in any part of the world. They welcomed the adoption of the Convention on the Suppression of Terrorist Bombings as the latest in the series of United Nations enactments on this subject and United Nations' Security Council Resolution 1269 of 19th October, 1999. They called for the adoption at the current session of the United Nations General Assembly, of the International Convention on the Suppression of Acts of Terrorist Financing, and welcomed the agreement on elaborating, on priority basis, a Comprehensive Convention Against International Terrorism. Recognising the linkages between terrorism, illegal trafficking in drugs, arms, and of persons, and money laundering, they further called on all states to enact laws to prevent financing of terrorists and terrorist organisations. They also called for firm deterrent measures by the United Nations Security Council against states, entities and organisations which harbour and train terrorists or promote international terrorism.

9

Resolution 1363 (2001) Adopted by the Security Council at its 4352nd meeting on 30 July 2001

The Security Council,

Reaffirming its previous resolutions, in particular resolution 1267 (1999) of 15 October 1999 and resolution 1333 (2000) of 19 December 2000, as well as the statements of its President on the situation in Afghanistan,

Determining that the situation in Afghanistan constitutes a threat to international peace and security in the region,

Acting under Chapter VII of the Charter of the United Nations,

1. *Stresses* the obligation under the Charter of the United Nations of all Member States to comply fully with the measures imposed by resolutions 1267 (1999) and 1333 (2000);

2. *Welcomes* the report (S/2001/511) of the Committee of Experts established pursuant to resolution 1333 (2000), and *notes* the conclusions and recommendations contained therein, following consultations with the States bordering the territory of Afghanistan under Taliban control which it had visited;

3. *Requests* the Secretary-General to establish, in consultation with the Committee established pursuant to resolution 1267 (1999), within 30 days of the date of adoption of this resolution and for a period running concurrently with the application of

the measures imposed by resolution 1333 (2000), a mechanism :

(a) to monitor the implementation of the measures imposed by resolutions 1267 (1999) and 1333 (2000);

(b) to offer assistance to States bordering the territory of Afghanistan under Taliban control and other States, as appropriate, to increase their capacity regarding the implementation of the measures imposed by resolutions 1267 (1999) and 1333 (2000); and

(c) to collate, assess, verify wherever possible, report and make recommendations on information regarding violations of the measures imposed by resolutions 1267 (1999) and 1333 (2000);

4. *Decides* that the composition of the monitoring mechanism, bearing in mind inter alia equitable geographical distribution, should be comprised of :

(a) a Monitoring Group in New York of up to five experts, including a Chairman, to monitor the implementation of all the measures imposed by resolutions 1267 (1999) and 1333 (2000), including in the fields of arms embargoes, counter-terrorism and related legislation and, in view of the link to the purchase of arms and financing of terrorism, money laundering, financial transactions and drug trafficking; and

(b) a Sanctions Enforcement Support Team, under the coordination of the Monitoring Group, of up to fifteen members with expertise in areas such as : customs, border security and counter-terrorism, to be located in those States referred to in paragraph 2 above, in full consultation and in close cooperation with those States;

5. *Requests* the Monitoring Group to report to the Committee established pursuant to resolution 1267 (1999) including through briefings of experts of the monitoring mechanism regarding the work of the monitoring mechanism as established in paragraph 3 above, and *requests also* the Sanctions Enforcement Support Team to report at least once a month to the Monitoring Group;

6. *Requests also* the Committee established pursuant to resolution 1267 (1999) to report to the Security Council on the implementation of this resolution at regular intervals;

7. *Calls upon* all States, the United Nations and concerned parties, to cooperate in a full and timely manner with the monitoring mechanism;

8. *Urges* all States to take immediate steps to enforce and strengthen through legislative enactments or administrative measures, where appropriate, the measures imposed under their domestic laws or regulations against their nationals and other individuals or entities operating on their territory, to prevent and punish violations of the measures imposed by resolutions 1267 (1999) and 1333 (2000), and to inform the Committee established pursuant to resolution 1267 (1999) of the adoption of such measures, and *invites* States to report the results of all related investigations or enforcement actions to the Committee unless to do so would compromise the investigation or enforcement action;

9. *Requests* the Secretary-General to make the necessary arrangements to support the work of the monitoring mechanism, as an expense of the Organization and through a United Nations Trust Fund established for this purpose, *affirms* that this Trust Fund will be established by the Secretary-General, *encourages* States to contribute to the Fund and to contribute, through the Secretary-General, personnel, equipment and services to the monitoring mechanism; and *further requests* the Secretary-General to keep the Committee established pursuant to resolution 1267 (1999) informed on a regular basis of the financial arrangements supporting the mechanism;

10. *Expresses* its intention to review the implementation of the measures imposed by resolutions 1267 (1999) and 1333 (2000) on the basis of the information provided by the monitoring mechanism through the Committee established pursuant to resolution 1267 (1999);

11. *Decides* to remain seized of the matter.

10

Resolution adopted by the General Assembly (30 January 2001)

[*on the report of the Sixth Committee (A/55/614)*]

55/158. Measures to eliminate international terrorism

The General Assembly,

Guided by the purposes and principles of the Charter of the United Nations,

Recalling all General Assembly and Security Council resolutions on measures to eliminate international terrorism,

Convinced of the importance of the consideration of measures to eliminate international terrorism by the General Assembly as the universal organ having competence to do so,

Recalling the Declaration on the Occasion of the Fiftieth Anniversary of the United Nations,[1]

Recalling also the United Nations Millennium Declaration,[2]

Deeply disturbed by the persistence of terrorist acts, which have been carried out worldwide,

Stressing the need to strengthen further international cooperation between States and between international organizations and agencies, regional organizations and arrangements and the United Nations in order to prevent, combat and eliminate terrorism in all its forms and manifestations, wherever and by whomsoever committed, in accordance with the principles of the Charter, international law and relevant international conventions,

Mindful of the need to enhance the role of the United Nations and the relevant specialized agencies in combating international terrorism, and of the proposals of the Secretary-General to enhance the role of the Organization in this respect,

Recalling the Declaration on Measures to Eliminate International Terrorism, contained in the annex to resolution 49/60 of 9 December 1994, wherein the General Assembly encouraged States to review urgently the scope of the existing international legal provisions on the prevention, repression and elimination of terrorism in all its forms and manifestations, with the aim of ensuring that there was a comprehensive legal framework covering all aspects of the matter,

Taking note of the final document of the Thirteenth Ministerial Conference of the Movement of Non-Aligned Countries, held at Cartagena, Colombia, on 8 and 9 April 2000,[3] which reiterated the collective position of the Movement of Non-Aligned Countries on terrorism and reaffirmed the previous initiative of the Twelfth Conference of Heads of State or Government of Non-Aligned Countries, held at Durban, South Africa, from 29 August to 3 September 1998, calling for an international summit conference under the auspices of the United Nations to formulate a joint organized response of the international community to terrorism in all its forms and manifestations,[4] and other relevant initiatives,

Recalling its decision in resolution 54/110 of 9 December 1999 that the Ad Hoc Committee established by General Assembly resolution 51/210 of 17 December 1996 should address the question of convening a high-level conference under the auspices of the United Nations to formulate a joint organized response of the international community to terrorism in all its forms and manifestations,

Noting regional efforts to prevent, combat and eliminate terrorism in all its forms and manifestations, wherever and by whomsoever committed, including through the elaboration of and adherence to regional conventions,

Having examined the report of the Secretary-General,[5] the report of the Ad Hoc Committee[6] and the report of the Working Group of the Sixth Committee established pursuant to resolution 54/110,[7]

1. *Strongly condemns* all acts, methods and practices of terrorism as criminal and unjustifiable, wherever and by whomsoever committed;

2. *Reiterates* that criminal acts intended or calculated to provoke a state of terror in the general public, a group of persons or particular persons for political purposes are in any circumstances unjustifiable, whatever the considerations of a political, philosophical, ideological, racial, ethnic, religious or other nature that may be invoked to justify them;

3. *Reiterates its call* upon all States to adopt further measures in accordance with the Charter of the United Nations and the relevant provisions of international law, including international standards of human rights, to prevent terrorism and to strengthen international cooperation in combating terrorism and, to that end, to consider in particular the implementation of the measures set out in paragraphs 3 (a) to (f) of resolution 51/210;

4. *Also reiterates its call* upon all States, with the aim of enhancing the efficient implementation of relevant legal instruments, to intensify, as and where appropriate, the exchange of information on facts related to terrorism and, in so doing, to avoid the dissemination of inaccurate or unverified information;

5. *Reiterates its call* upon States to refrain from financing, encouraging, providing training for or otherwise supporting terrorist activities;

6. *Reaffirms* that international cooperation as well as actions by States to combat terrorism should be conducted in conformity with the principles of the Charter, international law and relevant international conventions;

7. *Urges* all States that have not yet done so to consider, as a matter of priority, becoming parties to relevant conventions and protocols as referred to in paragraph 6 of resolution 51/210, as well as the International Convention for the Suppression of Terrorist Bombings,[8] and the International Convention for the Suppression of the Financing of Terrorism,[9] and calls upon all States to enact, as appropriate, domestic legislation necessary to implement the provisions of those conventions and protocols, to ensure that the jurisdiction of their courts enables them to bring to trial the perpetrators of terrorist acts, and to cooperate with and provide support and assistance to other States and relevant international and regional organizations to that end;

8. *Notes with appreciation and satisfaction* that, during the fifty-fourth session of the General Assembly and the Millennium Assembly, a number of States became parties to the relevant conventions and protocols referred to in paragraph 7 above, thereby realizing the objective of wider acceptance and implementation of those conventions;

9. *Reaffirms* the Declaration on Measures to Eliminate International Terrorism contained in the annex to resolution 49/60 and the Declaration to Supplement the 1994 Declaration on Measures to Eliminate International Terrorism contained in the annex to resolution 51/210, and calls upon all States to implement them;

10. *Welcomes* the efforts of the Terrorism Prevention Branch of the Centre for International Crime Prevention in Vienna, after reviewing existing possibilities within the United Nations system, to enhance, through its mandate, the capabilities of the United Nations in the prevention of terrorism;

11. *Invites* States that have not yet done so to submit to the Secretary-General information on their national laws and regulations regarding the prevention and suppression of acts of international terrorism;

12. *Invites* regional intergovernmental organizations to submit to the Secretary-General information on the measures

they have adopted at the regional level to eliminate international terrorism;

13. *Decides* that the Ad Hoc Committee established by General Assembly resolution 51/210 of 17 December 1996 shall continue to elaborate a comprehensive convention on international terrorism and shall continue its efforts to resolve the outstanding issues relating to the elaboration of a draft international convention for the suppression of acts of nuclear terrorism, as a means of further developing a comprehensive legal framework of conventions dealing with international terrorism, and that it shall keep on its agenda the question of convening a high-level conference under the auspices of the United Nations to formulate a joint organized response of the international community to terrorism in all its forms and manifestations;

14. *Also decides* that the Ad Hoc Committee shall meet from 12 to 23 February 2001 to continue the elaboration of a draft comprehensive convention on international terrorism, with appropriate time allocated to the continued consideration of outstanding issues relating to the elaboration of a draft international convention for the suppression of acts of nuclear terrorism, that it shall keep on its agenda the question of convening a high-level conference under the auspices of the United Nations to formulate a joint organized response of the international community to terrorism in all its forms and manifestations, and that the work shall continue during the fifty-sixth session of the General Assembly between 15 and 26 October 2001, within the framework of a working group of the Sixth Committee;

15. *Requests* the Secretary-General to continue to provide the Ad Hoc Committee with the necessary facilities for the performance of its work;

16. *Requests* the Ad Hoc Committee to report to the General Assembly at its fifty-fifth session in the event of the completion of the draft international convention for the suppression of acts of nuclear terrorism;

17. *Also requests* the Ad Hoc Committee to report to the General Assembly at its fifty-sixth session on progress made in the implementation of its mandate;

18. *Decides* to include in the provisional agenda of its fifty-sixth session the item entitled "Measures to eliminate international terrorism".

84th plenary meeting
12 December 2000

NOTES

1. See resolution 50/6.
2. See resolution 55/2.
3. A/54/917-S/2000/580, annex.
4. See A/53/667-S/1998/1071, annex I, paras. 149–162.
5. A/55/179 and Add.1.
6. *Official Records of the General Assembly, Fifty-fifth Session, Supplement No. 37* (A/55/37).
7. A/C.6/55/L.2.
8. Resolution 52/164, annex.
9. Resolution 54/109, annex.

11

Resolution 1333 (2000) Adopted by the Security Council at its 4251st meeting on 19 December 2000

The Security Council,

Reaffirming its previous resolutions, in particular resolution 1267 (1999) of 15 October 1999 and the statements of its President on the situation in Afghanistan,

Reaffirming its strong commitment to the sovereignty, independence, territorial integrity and national unity of Afghanistan, and its respect for Afghanistan's cultural and historical heritage,

Recognizing the critical humanitarian needs of the Afghan people,

Supporting the efforts of the Personal Representative of the Secretary-General for Afghanistan to advance a peace process through political negotiations between the Afghan parties aimed at the establishment of a broad-based, multi-ethnic, and fully representative government, and *calling for* the warring factions to cooperate fully with those efforts to conclude a ceasefire and begin discussions leading to a political settlement, by moving forward promptly in the process of dialogue to which they have committed themselves,

Noting the December 2000 meeting of the Afghan Support Group which emphasized that the situation in Afghanistan is a complex one that requires a comprehensive, integrated approach to a peace process and issues of narcotics trafficking, terrorism, human rights, and international humanitarian and development aid,

Recalling the relevant international counter-terrorism conventions and in particular the obligations of parties to those conventions to extradite or prosecute terrorists,

Strongly condemning the continuing use of the areas of Afghanistan under the control of the Afghan faction known as Taliban, which also calls itself the Islamic Emirate of Afghanistan (hereinafter known as the Taliban), for the sheltering and training of terrorists and planning of terrorist acts, and *reaffirming* its conviction that the suppression of international terrorism is essential for the maintenance of international peace and security,

Noting the importance of the Taliban acting in accordance with the 1961 Single Convention, the 1971 Convention on Psychotropic Substances, and the 1988 Convention against Illicit Traffic in Narcotic Drugs and Psychotropic Substances, and the commitments of the 1998 Twentieth Special Session of the General Assembly on Narcotic Drugs, including to work closely with the United Nations Drug Control Programme,

Noting that the Taliban benefits directly from the cultivation of illicit opium by imposing a tax on its production and indirectly benefits from the processing and trafficking of such opium, and *recognizing* that these substantial resources strengthen the Taliban's capacity to harbour terrorists,

Deploring the fact that the Taliban continues to provide safehaven to Usama bin Laden and to allow him and others associated with him to operate a network of terrorist training camps from Taliban-controlled territory and to use Afghanistan as a base from which to sponsor international terrorist operations,

Noting the indictment of Usama bin Laden and his associates by the United States of America for, inter alia, the 7 August 1998 bombings of the United States embassies in Nairobi, Kenya and Dar es Salaam, Tanzania and for conspiring to kill

American nationals outside the United States, and *noting also* the request of the United States of America to the Taliban to surrender them for trial (S/1999/1021),

Reiterating its deep concern over the continuing violations of international humanitarian law and of human rights, particularly discrimination against women and girls, and over the significant rise in the illicit production of opium,

Stressing that the capture by the Taliban of the Consulate-General of the Islamic Republic of Iran and the murder of Iranian diplomats and a journalist in Mazar-e-Sharif constituted flagrant violations of established international law,

Determining that the failure of the Taliban authorities to respond to the demands in paragraph 13 of resolution 1214 (1998) and in paragraph 2 of resolution 1267 (1999) constitutes a threat to international peace and security,

Stressing its determination to ensure respect for its resolutions,

Reaffirming the necessity for sanctions to contain adequate and effective exemptions to avoid adverse humanitarian consequences on the people of Afghanistan, and that they be structured in a way that will not impede, thwart of delay the work of international humanitarian assistance organizations or governmental relief agencies providing humanitarian assistance to the civilian population in the country,

Underlining the responsibility of the Taliban for the well-being of the population in the areas of Afghanistan under its control, and in this context *calling on* the Taliban to ensure the safe and unhindered access of relief personnel and aid to all those in need in the territory under their control,

Recalling the relevant principles contained in the Convention on the Safety of United Nations and Associated Personnel adopted by the General Assembly in its resolution 49/59 of 9 December 1994,

Acting under Chapter VII of the Charter of the United Nations,

1. *Demands* that the Taliban comply with resolution 1267 (1999) and, in particular, cease the provision of sanctuary and training for international terrorists and their organizations, take appropriate effective measures to ensure that the territory under its control is not used for terrorist installations and camps, or for the preparation or organization of terrorist acts against other States or their citizens, and cooperate with international efforts to bring indicted terrorists to justice;

2. *Demands also* that the Taliban comply without further delay with the demand of the Security Council in paragraph 2 of resolution 1267 (1999) that requires the Taliban to turn over Usama bin Laden to appropriate authorities in a country where he has been indicted, or to appropriate authorities in a country where he will be returned to such a country, or to appropriate authorities in a country where he will be arrested and effectively brought to justice;

3. *Demands further* that the Taliban should act swiftly to close all camps where terrorists are trained within the territory under its control, and *calls* for the confirmation of such closures by the United Nations, inter alia, through information made available to the United Nations by Member States in accordance with paragraph 19 below and through such other means as are necessary to assure compliance with this resolution;

4. *Reminds* all States of their obligation to implement strictly the measures imposed by paragraph 4 of resolution 1267 (1999);

5. *Decides* that all States shall :

(a) Prevent the direct or indirect supply, sale and transfer to the territory of Afghanistan under Taliban control as designated by the Committee established pursuant to resolution 1267 (1999), hereinafter known as the Committee, by their nationals or from their territories, or using their flag vessels or aircraft, or arms and related material of all types including weapons and ammunition, military vehicles and equipment, paramilitary equipment, and spare parts for the aforementioned;

(b) Prevent the direct or indirect sale, supply and transfer to the territory of Afghanistan under Taliban control, as designated by the Committee, by their nationals or from their territories, of technical advice, assistance, or training related to the military activities of the armed personnel under the control of the Taliban;

(c) Withdraw any of their officials, agents, advisers, and military personnel employed by contract or other arrangement present in Afghanistan to advise the Taliban on military or related security matters, and urge other nationals in this context to leave the country;

6. *Decides* that the measures imposed by paragraph 5 above shall not apply to supplies of non-lethal military equipment intended solely for humanitarian or protective use, and related technical assistance or training, as approved in advance by the Committee, and *affirms* that the measures imposed by paragraph 5 above do not apply to protective clothing, including flak jackets and military helmets, exported to Afghanistan by United Nations personnel, representatives of the media, and humanitarian workers for their personal use only;

7. *Urges* all States that maintain diplomatic relations with the Taliban to reduce significantly the number and level of the staff at Taliban missions and posts and restrict or control the movement within their territory of all such staff who remain; in the case of Taliban missions to international organizations, the host State may, as it deems necessary, consult the organization concerned on the measures required to implement this paragraph;

8. *Decides* that all States shall take further measures :

(a) To close immediately and completely all Taliban offices in their territories;

(b) To close immediately all offices of Ariana Afghan Airlines in their territories;

(c) To freeze without delay funds and other financial

assets of Usama bin Laden and individuals and entities associated with him as designated by the Committee, including those in the Al-Qaida organization, and including funds derived or generated from property owned or controlled directly or indirectly by Usama bin Laden and individuals and entities associated with him, and to ensure that neither they nor any other funds or financial resources are made available, by their nationals or by any persons within their territory, directly or indirectly for the benefit of Usama bin Laden, his associates or any entities owned or controlled, directly or indirectly, by Usama bin Laden or individuals and entities associated with him including the Al-Qaida organization and *requests* the Committee to maintain an updated list, based on information provided by States and regional organizations, of the individuals and entities designated as being associated with Usama bin Laden, including those in the Al-Qaida organization;

9. *Demands* that the Taliban, as well as others, halt all illegal drugs activities and work to virtually eliminate the illicit cultivation of opium poppy, the proceeds of which finance Taliban terrorist activities;

10. *Decides* that all States shall prevent the sale, supply or transfer, by their nationals or from their territories, of the chemical acetic anhydride to any person in the territory of Afghanistan under Taliban control as designated by the Committee or to any person for the purpose of any activity carried on in, or operated from, the territory under Taliban control as designated by the Committee;

11. *Decides also* that all States are required to deny any aircraft permission to take off from, land in or over-fly their territories if that aircraft has taken off from, or is destined to land at, a place in the territory of Afghanistan designated by the Committee as being under Taliban control, unless the particular flight has been approved in advance by the Committee on the grounds of humanitarian need, including religious

obligations such as the performance of the Hajj, or on the grounds that the flight promotes discussion of a peaceful resolution of the conflict in Afghanistan, or in likely to promote Taliban compliance with this resolution or with resolution 1267 (1999);

12. *Decides further* that the Committee shall maintain a list of approved organizations and governmental relief agencies which are providing humanitarian assistance to Afghanistan, including the United Nations and its agencies, governmental relief agencies providing humanitarian assistance, the International Committee of the Red Cross and non-governmental organizations as appropriate, that the prohibition imposed by paragraph 11 above shall not apply to humanitarian flights operated by, or on behalf of, organizations and governmental relief agencies on the list approved by the Committee, that the Committee shall keep the list under regular review, adding new organizations and governmental relief agencies as appropriate and that the Committee shall remove organizations and governmental agencies from the list if it decides that they are operating, or are likely to operate, flights for other than humanitarian purposes, and shall notify such organizations and governmental agencies immediately that any flights operated by them, or on their behalf, are thereby subject to the provisions of paragraph 11 above;

13. *Calls upon* the Taliban to ensure the safe and unhindered access of relief personnel and aid to all those in need in the territory under their control, and *underlines* that the Taliban must provide guarantees for the safety, security and freedom of movement for United Nations and associated humanitarian relief personnel;

14. *Urges* States to take steps to restrict the entry into or transit through their territory of all senior officials of the rank of Deputy Minister or higher in the Taliban, the equivalent rank of armed personnel under the control of the Taliban, and other senior advisers and dignitaries of the Taliban, unless those officials are travelling for humanitarian purposes, including

religious obligation such as the performance of the Hajj, or where the travel promotes discussion of a peaceful resolution of the conflict in Afghanistan or involves compliance with this resolution or resolution 1267 (1999);

15. *Requests* the Secretary-General in consultation with the Committee :

(a) To appoint a committee of experts to make recommendations to the Council within sixty days of the adoption of this resolution regarding how the arms embargo and the closure of terrorist training camps demanded in paragraphs 3 and 5 above can be monitored, including inter alia the use of information obtained by Member States through their national means and provided by them to the Secretary-General;

(b) To consult with relevant Member States to put into effect the measures imposed by this resolution and resolution 1267 (1999) and report the results of such consultations to the Council;

(c) To report on the implementation of the existing measures, assess problems in enforcing these measures, make recommendations for strengthening enforcement, and evaluate actions of the Taliban to come into compliance;

(d) To review the humanitarian implications of the measures imposed by this resolution and resolution 1267 (1999), and to report back to the Council within 90 days of the adoption of this resolution with an assessment and recommendations, to report at regular intervals thereafter on any humanitarian implications and to present a comprehensive report on this issue and any recommendations no later than 30 days prior to the expiration of these measures;

16. *Requests* the Committee to fulfil its mandate by undertaking the following tasks in addition to those set out in resolution 1267 (1999) :

(a) To establish and maintain updated lists based on information provided by States, regional, and international organizations of all points of entry and landing areas for aircraft within the territory of Afghanistan under control by the Taliban and to notify Member States of the contents of such lists;

(b) To establish and maintain updated lists, based on information provided by States and regional organizations, of individuals and entities designated as being associated with Usama bin Laden, in accordance with paragraph 8 (c) above;

(c) To give consideration to, and decide upon, requests for the exceptions set out in paragraphs 6 and 11 above;

(d) To establish no later than one month after the adoption of this resolution and maintain an updated list of approved organizations and governmental relief agencies which are providing humanitarian assistance to Afghanistan, in accordance with paragraph 12 above;

(e) To make relevant information regarding implementation of these measures publicly available through appropriate media, including through the improved use of information technology;

(f) To consider, where and when appropriate, a visit to countries in the region by the Chairman of the Committee and such other members as may be required to enhance the full and effective implementation of the measure imposed by this resolution and resolution 1267 (1999) with a view to urging States to comply with relevant Council resolutions;

(g) To make periodic reports to the Council on information submitted to it regarding this resolution and resolution 1267 (1999), including possible violations of the measures reported to the Committee and recommendations for strengthening the effectiveness of these measures;

17. *Calls upon* all States and all international and regional orgnizations, including the United Nations and its specialized agencies, to act strictly in accordance with the provisions of this resolution, notwithstanding the existence of any rights on obligations conferred or imposed by any international agreement or any contract entered into or any licence or permit granted prior to the date of coming into force of the measures imposed by paragraphs 5, 8, 10 and 11 above;

18. *Calls upon* States to bring proceedings against persons and entities within their jurisdiction that violate the measures imposed by paragraphs 5, 8, 10 and 11 above and to impose appropriate penalties;

19. *Calls upon* all States to cooperate fully with the Committee in the fulfilment of its tasks, including supplying such information as may be required by the Committee in pursuance of this resolution;

20. *Requests* all States to report to the Committee within 30 days of the coming into force of the measures imposed by paragraphs 5, 8, 10 and 11 above on the steps they have taken with a view to effectively implementing this resolution;

21. *Requests* the Secretariat to submit for consideration by the Committee information received from Governments and public sources on possible violations of the measures imposed by paragraphs 5, 8, 10 and 11 above;

22. *Decides* that the measures imposed by paragraphs 5, 8, 10 and 11 above shall come into force at 00.01 Eastern Standard Time, one month after the adoption of this resolution;

23. *Further decides* that the measures imposed by paragraphs 5, 8, 10 and 11 above are established for twelve months and that, at the end of this period, the Council will decide whether the Taliban has complied with paragraphs 1, 2 and 3 above, and, accordingly, whether to extend these measures for a further period with the same conditions;

24. *Decides* if the Taliban comply with the conditions of paragraphs 1, 2 and 3 above, before the twelve-month period

has elapsed, the Security Council shall terminate the measures imposed by paragraphs 5, 8, 10 and 11 above;

25. *Expresses* its readiness to consider the imposition of further measures, in accordance with its responsibility under the Charter of the United Nations, with the aim of achieving full implementation of this resolution and resolution 1267 (1999), inter alia, taking into account the impact assessment referred to in paragraph 15 (d) with a view to enhancing the effectiveness of sanctions and avoiding humanitarian consequences;

26. *Decides* to remain actively seized of the matter.

12

Statement by the President of the Security Council (6 December 2000)

At the 4243rd meeting of the Security Council, held on 6 December 2000, in connection with the Council's consideration of the item entitled "The responsibility of the Security Council in the maintenance of international peace and security", the President of the Security Council made the following statement on behalf of the Council :

"The Security Council takes note with appreciation of the briefing of Under-Secretary-General Mr. Hans Corell regarding follow-up measures to resolution 1269 (1999) of 19 October 1999.

"The Security Council is deeply concerned by the increase, in many regions of the world, of acts of terrorism in all its forms and manifestations. The Council reiterates its condemnation of all acts of terrorism, irrespective of motive, wherever and by whomever committed. It welcomes the efforts of the General Assembly and other organs of the United Nations in the field of combating international terrorism.

"The Security Council calls on all States that have not done so to consider, as a matter of priority, becoming party to the existing anti-terrorism conventions.

"The Security Council reaffirms its resolution 1269

(1999) of 19 October 1999 and calls upon all States to implement its provisions fully and expeditiously.

"The Security Council reiterates its readiness, including on the basis of the relevant reports of the Secretary-General, as provided for in its resolution 1269 (1999) of 19 October 1999, to take necessary steps in accordance with its responsibilities under the Charter of the United Nations in order to counter terrorist threats international peace and security.

"The Security Council will remain seized of this matter."

13

Statement by the President of the Security Council (7 April 2000)

At the 4125th meeting of the Security Council, held on 7 April 2000 in connection with the Council's consideration of the item entitled "The situation in Afghanistan", the President of the Security Council made the following statement on behalf of the Council :

> "The Security Council has considered the report of the Secretary-General concerning the situation in Afghanistan and its implications for international peace and security of 10 March 2000 (A/54/791-S/2000/205).
>
> "The Security Council reiterates its grave concern at the continued Afghan conflict, which is a serious and growing threat to regional and international peace and security. It strongly condemns the Taliban for the launching of new offensives, most notably that of 1 March 2000. The Council expresses its deep concern at the reports that both parties to the conflict are preparing for renewed large-scale fighting and recalls its repeated demands that the Afghan parties cease fighting. These events add to the enormous suffering of the civilian population of Afghanistan.
>
> "The Security Council reiterates that there is no military solution to the conflict in Afghanistan and that only a

negotiated political settlement aimed at the establishment of a broad-based, multi-ethnic and fully representative government acceptable to all Afghans can lead to peace and national reconciliation. It notes that the United Front of Afghanistan is willing to talk with the Taliban and recalls its demand that the parties, in particular the Taliban, resume negotiations under United Nations auspices without delay and preconditions in full compliance with the relevant resolutions of the General Assembly and the Council.

"The Security Council calls upon all Afghan parties to comply with their obligations under international humanitarian law and to ensure the full and unhindered access of international humanitarian assistance and personnel to all those in need. It expresses its grave concern at the further deterioration of the humanitarian situation in Afghanistan as a result of ongoing hostilities. The Taliban has the primary responsibility for this.

"The Security Councii strongly condemns the Taliban for the repeated forced entries on 26, 27 and 29 March 2000 by its armed groups into and searches of the United Nations premises in Kandahar and for the intimidation of the United Nations personnel. It stresses that responsibility for the subsequent withdrawal of all international staff from Kandahar and suspension of humanitarian assistance activities in southern Afghanistan rests solely with the Taliban. The Council demands that the Taliban stop these unacceptable practices and ensure the safety and security of all United Nations and associated personnel and humanitarian personnel working in Afghanistan in accordance with international law.

"The Security Council stresses its grave concern at the human rights situation in Afghanistan, which is unacceptable. It expresses particular alarm at the continuing disregard by the Taliban of the concerns expressed by the international community. The Council strongly condemns the forced displacement of the civilian population, notably that conducted by the Taliban in 1999, the deliberate targeting of civilians and the destruction of their assets and means of survival, summary executions, arbitrary detention of civilians and forced labour of those in detention, the separation of men from their families, indiscriminate bombing and other violations of human rights and international humanitarian law. It calls upon all Afghan parties, especially the Taliban, to put an end to such practices and to ensure the protection of civilians.

"The Security Council reaffirms the principle of non-refoulement of refugees, as provided for in relevant instruments of international law, welcomes recent efforts of countries neighbouring Afghanistan to support the voluntary repatriation of Afghan refugees in safety and dignity, and urges those host States to continue to provide international protection to Afghan refugees in need of it. It encourages the international community to provide the necessary assistance in this regard.

"The Security Council condemns the continuing grave violations of the human rights of women and girls, including all forms of discrimination against them, in all areas of Afghanistan, particularly in areas under the control of the Taliban. It remains deeply concerned about continued restrictions on their access to health care, to education and to employment outside the home, and about restrictions on their freedom of movement and freedom from intimidation, harassment and violence. The Council notes the recent reports of modest progress regarding the access of women and girls to certain services, but considers that such incremental improvements, while welcome, still fall far short of the minimum expectations of the international community, and calls upon all parties, particularly the Taliban, to take measures to end all violations of human rights of women and girls.

"The Security Council reiterates that outside interference in the internal affairs of Afghanistan, including the involvement of foreign combatants and military personnel and the supply of weapons and other materials used in the conflict, should cease immediately. It calls upon all States to take resolute measures to prohibit their military personnel from planning and participating in combat operations in Afghanistan, and immediately to withdraw their personnel and to assure that the supply of ammunition and other war-making materials is halted. The Council expresses its deep concern at the continuing involvement in the fighting in Afghanistan, on the side of the Taliban forces, of thousands of non-Afghan nationals.

"The Security Council reiterates its position that the United Nations must continue to play its central and impartial role in international efforts towards a peaceful resolution of the Afghan conflict. It welcomes the appointment of a new Personal Representative of the Secretary-General and the activities of the United Nations Special Mission to Afghanistan (UNSMA) to facilitate a political process aimed at achieving a lasting political settlement to the conflict. The Council supports the phased deployment of the UNSMA Civil Affairs Unit inside Afghanistan, as the security conditions permit.

"The Security Council welcomes the renewed commitment of members of the 'Six plus Two' group to contribute to a peaceful resolution of the Afghan conflict in support of the efforts of the United Nations, and urges the members of the group and the Afghan parties to implement the Tashkent Declaration on Fundamental Principles for a Peaceful Settlement of the Conflict in Afghanistan (A/54/174-S/1999/812, annex), particularly the agreement of members of the group not to provide military support to any Afghan party and to prevent the use of their territories for such purposes.

"The Security Council expresses its appreciation for the efforts undertaken by the Organization of the Islamic Conference, in support of and in coordination with the United Nations, to facilitate the convening of negotiations between the two Afghan parties. It encourages the process launched in Rome to convene a loya jirgah in Afghanistan and acknowledges other recent efforts to promote peace in Afghanistan, such as those of the Cyprus group and the meeting in Tokyo.

"The Security Council strongly condemns the continuing use of Afghan territory, especially areas controlled by the Taliban, for the sheltering and training of terrorists and planning of terrorist acts, and reaffirms its conviction that the suppression of international terrorism is essential for the maintenance of international peace and security. It insists that the Taliban cease the provision of sanctuary and training for international terrorists and their organizations, take effective measures to ensure that the territory under its control is not used for terrorist installations and camps or for the preparation or organization of terrorist acts against other States or their citizens, and cooperate with efforts to bring indicted terrorists to justice.

"The Security Council demands once again that the Taliban turn over indicted terrorist Usama bin Laden to appropriate authorities as set out in its resolution 1267 (1999) of 15 October 1999. It stresses that the continued failure of the Taliban to comply with this demand is unacceptable. The Council will ensure effective implementation of the measures imposed by that resolution. It condemns the recent attacks and planned attacks by terrorists affiliated with Usama bin Laden which constitute a continuing threat to the international community.

"The Security Council reiterates that the capture by the Taliban of the Consulate-General of the Islamic Republic of Iran and the murder of the Iranian diplomats and journalist in Mazar-e-Sharif as well as the murders of the United Nations personnel constitute flagrant violations of international law. It expresses its concern at the failure of the Taliban effectively to bring to justice those responsible for these crimes. The Council reiterates its demand that the Taliban cooperate fully with the United Nations in this regard.

"The Security Council is deeply disturbed by an alarming increase in the cultivation, production and trafficking of drugs in Afghanistan, especially in areas controlled by the Taliban, and by its consequences for the continuation of the conflict. It demands that the Taliban, as well as others, halt all illegal drugs activities. The Council encourages the initiative of the 'Six plus Two' group to address the drug-related issues in a coordinated manner with the support of the Office for Drug Control and Crime Prevention. It also encourages Member States and others concerned to increase their support for the efforts aimed at strengthening the drug control capacities of countries bordering Afghanistan.

"The Security Council stresses the need for prompt and effective implementation by all Member States of the measures imposed by its resolution 1267 (1999), and reminds Member States of their obligations under this resolution, including assisting in the identification of Taliban assets and aircraft. It underlines that sanctions are not aimed at the Afghan people, but are imposed against the Taliban because of its non-compliance with that resolution. The Council reaffirms its decision to assess the impact, including the humanitarian implications, of the measures imposed by that resolution. It encourages the Committee established pursuant to its resolution 1267 (1999) to report in this respect as soon as practicable.

"The Security Council holds the leadership of the Taliban responsible for not taking measures to comply with the demands made in its resolutions, especially to conclude a ceasefire and to resume negotiations, and stresses the need for the Taliban to comply with these demands without delay.

"In this context the Security Council reaffirms its readiness to consider the imposition of further targeted measures, in accordance with its responsibility under the Charter of the United Nations, with the aim of achieving the full implementation of all its relevant resolutions."

14

Resolution Adopted by the General Assembly (25 February 2000)

[on the report of the Sixth Committee (A/54/615)]

54/109. International Convention for the Suppression of the Financing of Terrorism

The General Assembly,

Recalling all its relevant resolutions, including resolution 46/51 of 9 December 1991, resolution 49/60 of 9 December 1994, by which it adopted the Declaration on Measures to Eliminate International Terrorism, and resolutions 51/210 of 17 December 1996 and 53/108 of 8 December 1998,

Having considered the text of the draft international convention for the suppression of the financing of terrorism prepared by the Ad Hoc Committee established by General Assembly resolution 51/210 of 17 December 1996 and the Working Group of the Sixth Committee,[1]

1. *Adopts* the International Convention for the Suppression of the Financing of Terrorism annexed to the present resolution, and requests the Secretary-General to open it for signature at United Nations Headquarters in New York from 10 January 2000 to 31 December 2001;

2. *Urges* all States to sign and ratify, accept, approve or accede to the Convention.

76th plenary meeting
9 December 1999

ANNEX

International Convention for the Suppression of the Financing of Terrorism

Preamble

The States Parties to this Convention,

Bearing in mind the purposes and principles of the Charter of the United Nations concerning the maintenance of international peace and security and the promotion of good-neighbourliness and friendly relations and cooperation among States,

Deeply concerned about the worldwide escalation of acts of terrorism in all its forms and manifestations,

Recalling the Declaration on the Occasion of the Fiftieth Anniversary of the United Nations, contained in General Assembly resolution 50/6 of 24 October 1995,

Recalling also all the relevant General Assembly resolutions on the matter, including resolution 49/60 of 9 December 1994 and the annex thereto on the Declaration on Measures to Eliminate International Terrorism, in which the States Members of the United Nations solemnly reaffirmed their unequivocal condemnation of all acts, methods and practices of terrorism as criminal and unjustifiable, wherever and by whomever committed, including those which jeopardize the friendly relations among States and peoples and threaten the territorial integrity and security of States,

Noting that the Declaration on Measures to Eliminate International Terrorism also encouraged States to review urgently the scope of the existing international legal provisions on the prevention, repression and elimination of terrorism in all its forms and manifestations, with the aim of ensuring that there is a comprehensive legal framework covering all aspects of the matter,

Recalling paragraph 3 (*f*) of General Assembly resolution 51/210 of 17 December 1996, in which the Assembly called upon all States to take steps to prevent and counteract, through appropriate domestic measures, the financing of terrorists and terrorist organizations, whether such financing is direct or indirect through organizations which also have or claim to have charitable, social or cultural goals or which are also engaged in unlawful activities such as illicit arms trafficking, drug dealing and racketeering, including the exploitation of persons for purposes of funding terrorist activities, and in particular to consider, where appropriate, adopting regulatory measures to prevent and counteract movements of funds suspected to be intended for terrorist purposes without impeding in any way the freedom of legitimate capital movements and to intensify the exchange of information concerning international movements of such funds,

Recalling also General Assembly resolution 52/165 of 15 December 1997, in which the Assembly called upon States to consider, in particular, the implementation of the measures set out in paragraphs 3 (*a*) to (*f*) of its resolution 51/210,

Recalling further General Assembly resolution 53/108 of 8 December 1998, in which the Assembly decided that the Ad Hoc Committee established by General Assembly resolution 51/210 of 17 December 1996 should elaborate a draft international convention for the suppression of terrorist financing to supplement related existing international instruments,

Considering that the financing of terrorism is a matter of grave concern to the international community as a whole,

Noting that the number and seriousness of acts of international terrorism depend on the financing that terrorists may obtain,

Noting also that existing multilateral legal instruments do not expressly address such financing,

Being convinced of the urgent need to enhance international cooperation among States in devising and adopting effective measures for the prevention of the financing of terrorism, as well as for its suppression through the prosecution and punishment of its perpetrators,

Have agreed as follows :

Article 1

For the purposes of this Convention :

1. "Funds" means assets of every kind, whether tangible or intangible, movable or immovable, however acquired, and legal documents or instruments in any form, including electronic or digital, evidencing title to, or interest in, such assets, including, but not limited to, bank credits, travellers cheques, bank cheques, money orders, shares, securities, bonds, drafts and letters of credit.

2. "State or government facility" means any permanent or temporary facility or conveyance that is used or occupied by representatives of a State, members of Government, the legislature or the judiciary or by officials or employees of a State or any other public authority or entity or by employees or officials of an intergovernmental organization in connection with their official duties.

3. "Proceeds" means any funds derived from or obtained, directly or indirectly, through the commission of an offence set forth in article 2.

Article 2

1. Any person commits an offence within the meaning of this Convention if that person by any means, directly or indirectly, unlawfully and wilfully, provides or collects funds with the intention that they should be used or in the knowledge that they are to be used, in full or in part, in order to carry out :

(a) An act which constitutes an offence within the scope of and as defined in one of the treaties listed in the annex; or

(b) Any other act intended to cause death or serious bodily injury to a civilian, or to any other person not taking an active part in the hostilities in a situation of armed conflict, when the purpose of such act, by its nature or context, is to intimidate a population, or to compel a Government or an international organization to do or to abstain from doing any act.

2. (a) On depositing its instrument of ratification, acceptance, approval or accession, a State Party which is not a party to a treaty listed in the annex may declare that, in the application of this Convention to the State Party, the treaty shall be deemed not to be included in the annex referred to in paragraph 1, subparagraph (*a*).

The declaration shall cease to have effect as soon as the treaty enters into force for the State Party, which shall notify the depositary of this fact;

(b) When a State Party ceases to be a party to a treaty listed in the annex, it may make a declaration as provided for in this article, with respect to that treaty.

3. For an act to constitute an offence set forth in paragraph 1, it shall not be necessary that the funds were actually used to carry out an offence referred to in paragraph 1, subparagraph (a) or (b).

4. Any person also commits an offence if that person attempts to commit an offence as set forth in paragraph 1 of this article.

5. Any person also commits an offence if that person :

(a) Participates as an accomplice in an offence as set forth in paragraph 1 or 4 of this article;

(b) Organizes or directs others to commit an offence as set forth in paragraph 1 or 4 of this article;

(c) Contributes to the commission of one or more offences as set forth in paragraph 1 or 4 of this article by a group of persons acting with a common purpose. Such contribution shall be intentional and shall either :

(i) Be made with the aim of furthering the criminal activity or criminal purpose of the group, where such activity or purpose involves the commission of an offence as set forth in paragraph 1 of this article; or

(ii) Be made in the knowledge of the intention of the group to commit an offence as set forth in paragraph 1 of this article.

Article 3

This Convention shall not apply where the offence is committed within a single State, the alleged offender is a national of that State and is present in the territory of that State and no other State has a basis under article 7, paragraph 1 or 2, to exercise jurisdiction, except that the provisions of articles 12 to 18 shall, as appropriate, apply in those cases.

Article 4

Each State Party shall adopt such measures as may be necessary :

(a) To establish as criminal offences under its domestic law the offences as set forth in article 2;

(b) To make those offences punishable by appropriate penalties which take into account the grave nature of the offences.

Article 5

1. Each State Party, in accordance with its domestic legal principles, shall take the necessary measures to enable a legal entity located in its territory or organized under its laws to be held liable when a person responsible for the management or control of that legal entity has, in that capacity, committed an offence as set forth in article 2. Such liability may be criminal, civil or administrative.

2. Such liability is incurred without prejudice to the criminal liability of individuals who have committed the offences.

3. Each State Party shall ensure, in particular, that legal entities liable in accordance with paragraph 1 above are subject to effective, proportionate and dissuasive criminal, civil or administrative sanctions. Such sanctions may include monetary sanctions.

Article 6

Each State Party shall adopt such measures as may be necessary, including, where appropriate, domestic legislation, to ensure that criminal acts within the scope of this Convention are under no circumstances justifiable by considerations of a political, philosophical, ideological, racial, ethnic, religious or other similar nature.

Article 7

1. Each State Party shall take such measures as may be necessary to establish its jurisdiction over the offences set forth in article 2 when :

(a) The offence is committed in the territory of that State;

(b) The offence is committed on board a vessel flying the flag of that State or an aircraft registered under the laws of that State at the time the offence is committed;

(c) The offence is committed by a national of that State.

2. A State Party may also establish its jurisdiction over any such offence when :

(a) The offence was directed towards or resulted in the carrying out of an offence referred to in article 2, paragraph 1, subparagraph (a) or (b), in the territory of or against a national of that State;

(b) The offence was directed towards or resulted in the carrying out of an offence referred to in article 2, paragraph 1, subparagraph (a) or (b), against a State or government facility of that State abroad, including diplomatic or consular premises of that State;

(c) The offence was directed towards or resulted in an offence referred to in article 2, paragraph 1, subparagraph (a) or (b), committed in an attempt to compel that State to do or abstain from doing any act;

(d) The offence is committed by a stateless person who has his or her habitual residence in the territory of that State;

(e) The offence is committed on board an aircraft which is operated by the Government of that State.

3. Upon ratifying, accepting, approving or acceding to this Convention, each State Party shall notify the Secretary-General of the United Nations of the jurisdiction it has established in accordance with paragraph 2. Should any change take place, the State Party concerned shall immediately notify the Secretary-General.

4. Each State Party shall likewise take such measures as may be necessary to establish its jurisdiction over the offences set forth in article 2 in cases where the alleged offender is present in its territory and it does not extradite that person to any of the States Parties that have established their jurisdiction in accordance with paragraphs 1 or 2.

5. When more than one State Party claims jurisdiction over the offences set forth in article 2, the relevant States Parties shall strive to coordinate their actions appropriately, in particular concerning the conditions for prosecution and the modalities for mutual legal assistance.

6. Without prejudice to the norms of general international law, this Convention does not exclude the exercise of any criminal jurisdiction established by a State Party in accordance with its domestic law.

Article 8

1. Each State Party shall take appropriate measures, in accordance with its domestic legal principles, for the identification, detection and freezing or seizure of any funds used or allocated for the purpose of committing the offences set forth in article 2 as well as the proceeds derived from such offences, for purposes of possible forfeiture.

2. Each State Party shall take appropriate measures, in accordance with its domestic legal principles, for the forfeiture of funds used or allocated for the purpose of committing the offences set forth in article 2 and the proceeds derived from such offences.

3. Each State Party concerned may give consideration to concluding agreements on the sharing with other States Parties, on a regular or case-by-case basis, of the funds derived from the forfeitures referred to in this article.

4. Each State Party shall consider establishing mechanisms whereby the funds derived from the forfeitures referred to in this article are utilized to compensate the victims of offences referred to in article 2, paragraph 1, subparagraph (a) or (b), or their families.

5. The provisions of this article shall be implemented without prejudice to the rights of third parties acting in good faith.

Article 9

1. Upon receiving information that a person who has committed or who is alleged to have committed an offence set forth in article 2 may be present in its territory, the State Party concerned shall take such measures as may be necessary under its domestic law to investigate the facts contained in the information.

2. Upon being satisfied that the circumstances so warrant, the State Party in whose territory the offender or alleged offender is present shall take the appropriate measures under its domestic law so as to ensure that person's presence for the purpose of prosecution or extradition.

3. Any person regarding whom the measures referred to in paragraph 2 are being taken shall be entitled :

(a) To communicate without delay with the nearest appropriate representative of the State of which that person is a national or which is otherwise entitled to protect that person's rights or, if that person is a stateless person, the State in the territory of which that person habitually resides;

(b) To be visited by a representative of that State;

(c) To be informed of that person's rights under subparagraphs (a) and (b).

4. The rights referred to in paragraph 3 shall be exercised in conformity with the laws and regulations of the State in the territory of which the offender or alleged offender is present, subject to the provision that the said laws and regulations must enable full effect to be given to the purposes for which the rights accorded under paragraph 3 are intended.

5. The provisions of paragraphs 3 and 4 shall be without prejudice to the right of any State Party having a claim to jurisdiction in accordance with article 7, paragraph 1, subparagraph (b), or paragraph 2, subparagraph (b), to invite the International Committee of the Red Cross to communicate with and visit the alleged offender.

6. When a State Party, pursuant to the present article, has taken a person into custody, it shall immediately notify, directly or through the Secretary-General of the United Nations, the States Parties which have established jurisdiction in accordance with article 7, paragraph 1 or 2, and, if it considers it advisable, any other interested States Parties, of the fact that such person is in custody and of the circumstances which warrant that person's detention. The State which makes the investigation contemplated in paragraph 1 shall promptly inform the said States Parties of its findings and shall indicate whether it intends to exercise jurisdiction.

Article 10

1. The State Party in the territory of which the alleged offender is present shall, in cases to which article 7 applies, if it does not extradite that person, be obliged, without exception whatsoever and whether or not the offence was committed in its territory, to submit the case without undue delay to its competent authorities for the purpose of prosecution, through proceedings in accordance with the laws of that State. Those authorities shall take their decision in the same manner as in the case of any other offence of a grave nature under the law of that State.

2. Whenever a State Party is permitted under its domestic

law to extradite or otherwise surrender one of its nationals only upon the condition that the person will be returned to that State to serve the sentence imposed as a result of the trial or proceeding for which the extradition or surrender of the person was sought, and this State and the State seeking the extradition of the person agree with this option and other terms they may deem appropriate, such a conditional extradition or surrender shall be sufficient to discharge the obligation set forth in paragraph 1.

Article 11

1. The offences set forth in article 2 shall be deemed to be included as extraditable offences in any extradition treaty existing between any of the States Parties before the entry into force of this Convention. States Parties undertake to include such offences as extraditable offences in every extradition treaty to be subsequently concluded between them.

2. When a State Party which makes extradition conditional on the existence of a treaty receives a request for extradition from another State Party with which it has no extradition treaty, the requested State Party may, at its option, consider this Convention as a legal basis for extradition in respect of the offences set forth in article 2. Extradition shall be subject to the other conditions provided by the law of the requested State.

3. States Parties which do not make extradition conditional on the existence of a treaty shall recognize the offences set forth in article 2 as extraditable offences between themselves, subject to the conditions provided by the law of the requested State.

4. If necessary, the offences set forth in article 2 shall be treated, for the purposes of extradition between States Parties, as if they had been committed not only in the place in which they occurred but also in the territory of the States that have established jurisdiction in accordance with article 7, paragraphs 1 and 2.

5. The provisions of all extradition treaties and arrangements

between States Parties with regard to offences set forth in article 2 shall be deemed to be modified as between States Parties to the extent that they are incompatible with this Convention.

Article 12

1. States Parties shall afford one another the greatest measure of assistance in connection with criminal investigations or criminal or extradition proceedings in respect of the offences set forth in article 2, including assistance in obtaining evidence in their possession necessary for the proceedings.

2. States Parties may not refuse a request for mutual legal assistance on the ground of bank secrecy.

3. The requesting Party shall not transmit or use information or evidence furnished by the requested Party for investigations, prosecutions or proceedings other than those stated in the request without the prior consent of the requested Party.

4. Each State Party may give consideration to establishing mechanisms to share with other States Parties information or evidence needed to establish criminal, civil or administrative liability pursuant to article 5.

5. States Parties shall carry out their obligations under paragraphs 1 and 2 in conformity with any treaties or other arrangements on mutual legal assistance or information exchange that may exist between them. In the absence of such treaties or arrangements, States Parties shall afford one another assistance in accordance with their domestic law.

Article 13

None of the offences set forth in article 2 shall be regarded, for the purposes of extradition or mutual legal assistance, as a fiscal offence. Accordingly, States Parties may not refuse a request for extradition or for mutual legal assistance on the sole ground that it concerns a fiscal offence.

Article 14

None of the offences set forth in article 2 shall be regarded for the purposes of extradition or mutual legal assistance as a political offence or as an offence connected with a political offence or as an offence inspired by political motives. Accordingly, a request for extradition or for mutual legal assistance based on such an offence may not be refused on the sole ground that it concerns a political offence or an offence connected with a political offence or an offence inspired by political motives.

Article 15

Nothing in this Convention shall be interpreted as imposing an obligation to extradite or to afford mutual legal assistance, if the requested State Party has substantial grounds for believing that the request for extradition for offences set forth in article 2 or for mutual legal assistance with respect to such offences has been made for the purpose of prosecuting or punishing a person on account of that person's race, religion, nationality, ethnic origin or political opinion or that compliance with the request would cause prejudice to that person's position for any of these reasons.

Article 16

1. A person who is being detained or is serving a sentence in the territory of one State Party whose presence in another State Party is requested for purposes of identification, testimony or otherwise providing assistance in obtaining evidence for the investigation or prosecution of offences set forth in article 2 may be transferred if the following conditions are met :

(a) The person freely gives his or her informed consent;

(b) The competent authorities of both States agree, subject to such conditions as those States may deem appropriate.

2. For the purposes of the present article :

(a) The State to which the person is transferred shall have the authority and obligation to keep the person transferred in custody, unless otherwise requested or authorized by the State from which the person was transferred;

(b) The State to which the person is transferred shall without delay implement its obligation to return the person to the custody of the State from which the person was transferred as agreed beforehand, or as otherwise agreed, by the competent authorities of both States;

(c) The State to which the person is transferred shall not require the State from which the person was transferred to initiate extradition proceedings for the return of the person;

(d) The person transferred shall receive credit for service of the sentence being served in the State from which he or she was transferred for time spent in the custody of the State to which he or she was transferred.

3. Unless the State Party from which a person is to be transferred in accordance with the present article so agrees, that person, whatever his or her nationality, shall not be prosecuted or detained or subjected to any other restriction of his or her personal liberty in the territory of the State to which that person is transferred in respect of acts or convictions anterior to his or her departure from the territory of the State from which such person was transferred.

Article 17

Any person who is taken into custody or regarding whom any other measures are taken or proceedings are carried out pursuant to this Convention shall be guaranteed fair treatment, including enjoyment of all rights and guarantees in conformity with the law of the State in the territory of which that person is present and applicable provisions of international law, including international human rights law.

Article 18

1. States Parties shall cooperate in the prevention of the

offences set forth in article 2 by taking all practicable measures, *inter alia*, by adapting their domestic legislation, if necessary, to prevent and counter preparations in their respective territories for the commission of those offences within or outside their territories, including :

(a) Measures to prohibit in their territories illegal activities of persons and organizations that knowingly encourage, instigate, organize or engage in the commission of offences set forth in article 2;

(b) Measures requiring financial institutions and other professions involved in financial transactions to utilize the most efficient measures available for the identification of their usual or occasional customers, as well as customers in whose interest accounts are opened, and to pay special attention to unusual or suspicious transactions and report transactions suspected of stemming from a criminal activity. For this purpose, States Parties shall consider :

(i) Adopting regulations prohibiting the opening of accounts, the holders or beneficiaries of which are unidentified or unidentifiable, and measures to ensure that such institutions verify the identity of the real owners of such transactions;

(ii) With respect to the identification of legal entities, requiring financial institutions, when necessary, to take measures to verify the legal existence and the structure of the customer by obtaining, either from a public register or from the customer or both, proof of incorporation, including information concerning the customer's name, legal form, address, directors and provisions regulating the power to bind the entity;

(iii) Adopting regulations imposing on financial institutions the obligation to report promptly to the competent authorities all complex, unusual large transactions and unusual patterns of transactions, which have no apparent economic or obviously lawful purpose, without fear of assuming criminal or civil liability for breach of any restriction on disclosure of information if they report their suspicions in good faith;

(iv) Requiring financial institutions to maintain, for at least five years, all necessary records on transactions, both domestic and international.

2. States Parties shall further cooperate in the prevention of offences set forth in article 2 by considering :

(a) Measures for the supervision, including, for example, the licensing, of all money-transmission agencies;

(b) Feasible measures to detect or monitor the physical cross-border transportation of cash and bearer negotiable instruments, subject to strict safeguards to ensure proper use of information and without impeding in any way the freedom of capital movements.

3. States Parties shall further cooperate in the prevention of the offences set forth in article 2 by exchanging accurate and verified information in accordance with their domestic law and coordinating administrative and other measures taken, as appropriate, to prevent the commission of offences set forth in article 2, in particular by :

(a) Establishing and maintaining channels of communication between their competent agencies and services to facilitate the secure and rapid exchange of information concerning all aspects of offences set forth in article 2;

(b) Cooperating with one another in conducting inquiries, with respect to the offences set forth in article 2, concerning :

(i) The identity, whereabouts and activities of persons in respect of whom reasonable suspicion exists that they are involved in such offences;

(ii) The movement of funds relating to the commission of such offences.

4. States Parties may exchange information through the International Criminal Police Organization (Interpol).

Article 19

The State Party where the alleged offender is prosecuted shall, in accordance with its domestic law or applicable procedures, communicate the final outcome of the proceedings to the Secretary-General of the United Nations, who shall transmit the information to the other States Parties.

Article 20

The States Parties shall carry out their obligations under this Convention in a manner consistent with the principles of sovereign equality and territorial integrity of States and that of non-intervention in the domestic affairs of other States.

Article 21

Nothing in this Convention shall affect other rights, obligations and responsibilities of States and individuals under international law, in particular the purposes of the Charter of the United Nations, international humanitarian law and other relevant conventions.

Article 22

Nothing in this Convention entitles a State Party to undertake in the territory of another State Party the exercise of jurisdiction or performance of functions which are exclusively reserved for the authorities of that other State Party by its domestic law.

Article 23

1. The annex may be amended by the addition of relevant treaties :

(a) That are open to the participation of all States;

(b) That have entered into force;

(c) That have been ratified, accepted, approved or acceded

to by at least twenty-two States Parties to the present Convention.

2. After the entry into force of this Convention, any State Party may propose such an amendment. Any proposal for an amendment shall be communicated to the depositary in written form. The depositary shall notify proposals that meet the requirements of paragraph 1 to all States Parties and seek their views on whether the proposed amendment should be adopted.

3. The proposed amendment shall be deemed adopted unless one third of the States Parties object to it by a written notification not later than 180 days after its circulation.

4. The adopted amendment to the annex shall enter into force 30 days after the deposit of the twenty-second instrument of ratification, acceptance or approval of such amendment for all those States Parties that have deposited such an instrument. For each State Party ratifying, accepting or approving the amendment after the deposit of the twenty-second instrument, the amendment shall enter into force on the thirtieth day after deposit by such State Party of its instrument of ratification, acceptance or approval.

Article 24

1. Any dispute between two or more States Parties concerning the interpretation or application of this Convention which cannot be settled through negotiation within a reasonable time shall, at the request of one of them, be submitted to arbitration. If, within six months from the date of the request for arbitration, the parties are unable to agree on the organization of the arbitration, any one of those parties may refer the dispute to the International Court of Justice, by application, in conformity with the Statute of the Court.

2. Each State may at the time of signature, ratification, acceptance or approval of this Convention or accession thereto declare that it does not consider itself bound by paragraph 1. The other States Parties shall not be bound by paragraph 1 with respect to any State Party which has made such a reservation.

3. Any State which has made a reservation in accordance with paragraph 2 may at any time withdraw that reservation by notification to the Secretary-General of the United Nations.

Article 25

1. This Convention shall be open for signature by all States from 10 January 2000 to 31 December 2001 at United Nations Headquarters in New York.

2. This Convention is subject to ratification, acceptance or approval. The instruments of ratification, acceptance or approval shall be deposited with the Secretary-General of the United Nations.

3. This Convention shall be open to accession by any State. The instruments of accession shall be deposited with the Secretary-General of the United Nations.

Article 26

1. This Convention shall enter into force on the thirtieth day following the date of the deposit of the twenty-second instrument of ratification, acceptance, approval or accession with the Secretary-General of the United Nations.

2. For each State ratifying, accepting, approving or acceding to the Convention after the deposit of the twenty-second instrument of ratification, acceptance, approval or accession, the Convention shall enter into force on the thirtieth day after deposit by such State of its instrument of ratification, acceptance, approval or accession.

Article 27

1. Any State Party may denounce this Convention by written notification to the Secretary-General of the United Nations.

2. Denunciation shall take effect one year following the date on which notification is received by the Secretary-General of the United Nations.

Article 28

The original of this Convention, of which the Arabic, Chinese, English, French, Russian and Spanish texts are equally authentic, shall be deposited with the Secretary-General of the United Nations who shall send certified copies thereof to all States.

IN WITNESS WHEREOF, the undersigned, being duly authorized thereto by their respective Governments, have signed this Convention, opened for signature at United Nations Headquarters in New York on 10 January 2000.

ANNEX

1. Convention for the Suppression of Unlawful Seizure of Aircraft, done at The Hague on 16 December 1970.
2. Convention for the Suppression of Unlawful Acts against the Safety of Civil Aviation, done at Montreal on 23 September 1971.
3. Convention on the Prevention and Punishment of Crimes against Internationally Protected Persons, including Diplomatic Agents, adopted by the General Assembly of the United Nations on 14 December 1973.
4. International Convention against the Taking of Hostages, adopted by the General Assembly of the United Nations on 17 December 1979.
5. Convention on the Physical Protection of Nuclear Material, adopted at Vienna on 3 March 1980.
6. Protocol for the Suppression of Unlawful Acts of Violence at Airports Serving International Civil Aviation, supplementary to the Convention for the Suppression of Unlawful Acts against the Safety of Civil Aviation, done at Montreal on 24 February 1988.
7. Convention for the Suppression of Unlawful Acts against the Safety of Maritime Navigation, done at Rome on 10 March 1988.

8. Protocol for the Suppression of Unlawful Acts against the Safety of Fixed Platforms located on the Continental Shelf, done at Rome on 10 March 1988.
9. International Convention for the Suppression of Terrorist Bombings, adopted by the General Assembly of the United Nations on 15 December 1997.

NOTE

1. A/C.6/54/L.2, annex I.

15

Resolution Adopted by the General Assembly (24 February 2000)

[*on the report of the Third Committee* (*A/54/605/Add.2*)]

54/164. Human rights and terrorism

The General Assembly,

Guided by the Charter of the United Nations, the Universal Declaration of Human Rights,[1] the Declaration on Principles of International Law concerning Friendly Relations and Cooperation among States in accordance with the Charter of the United Nations[2] and the International Covenants on Human Rights,[3]

Recalling the Declaration on the Occasion of the Fiftieth Anniversary of the United Nations,[4]

Recalling also the Vienna Declaration and Programme of Action adopted by the World Conference on Human Rights on 25 June 1993,[5] in which the Conference reaffirmed that terrorism is indeed aimed at the destruction of human rights, fundamental freedoms and democracy,

Recalling further its resolutions 48/122 of 20 December 1993, 49/185 of 23 December 1994, 50/186 of 22 December 1995 and 52/133 of 12 December 1997,

Recalling in particular its resolution 52/133, in which it requested the Secretary-General to seek the views of Member States on the implications of terrorism, in all its forms and manifestations, for the full enjoyment of human rights and fundamental freedoms,

Recalling previous resolutions of the Commission on Human Rights, and taking note, in particular, of resolution 1999/27 of 26 April 1999,[6] as well as the relevant resolutions of the Subcommission on the Promotion and Protection of Human Rights,[7]

Alarmed that acts of terrorism in all its forms and manifestations aimed at the destruction of human rights have continued despite national and international efforts,

Bearing in mind that the essential and most basic human right is the right to life,

Bearing in mind also that terrorism creates an environment that destroys the right of people to live in freedom from fear,

Reiterating that all States have an obligation to promote and protect all human rights and fundamental freedoms and that every individual should strive to secure their universal and effective recognition and observance,

Seriously concerned about the gross violations of human rights perpetrated by terrorist groups,

Profoundly deploring the increasing number of innocent persons, including women, children and the elderly, killed, massacred and maimed by terrorists in indiscriminate and random acts of violence and terror, which cannot be justified under any circumstances,

Noting with great concern the growing connection between the terrorist groups and other criminal organizations engaged in the illegal traffic in arms and drugs at the national and international levels, as well as the consequent commission of serious crimes such as murder, extortion, kidnapping, assault, the taking of hostages and robbery,

Emphasizing the importance of Member States taking appropriate steps to deny safe haven to those who plan, finance or commit terrorist acts, by ensuring their apprehension and prosecution or extradition,

Mindful of the need to protect the human rights of and guarantees for the individual in accordance with the relevant human rights principles and instruments, in particular the right to life,

Reaffirming that all measures to counter terrorism must be in strict conformity with the relevant provisions of international law including international human rights standards,

1. *Expresses its solidarity* with the victims of terrorism;

2. *Condemns* the violations of the right to live free from fear and of the right to life, liberty and security;

3. *Reiterates its unequivocal condemnation* of the acts, methods and practices of terrorism, in all its forms and manifestations, as activities aimed at the destruction of human rights, fundamental freedoms and democracy, threatening the territorial integrity and security of States, destabilizing legitimately constituted Governments, undermining pluralistic civil society and having adverse consequences for the economic and social development of States;

4. *Calls upon* States to take all necessary and effective measures in accordance with relevant provisions of international law, including international human rights standards, to prevent, combat and eliminate terrorism in all its forms and manifestations, wherever and by whomever committed;

5. *Urges* the international community to enhance cooperation at the regional and international levels in the fight against terrorism, in accordance with relevant international instruments, including those relating to human rights, with the aim of its eradication;

6. *Condemns* the incitement of ethnic hatred, violence and terrorism;

7. *Commends* those Governments that have communicated their views on the implications of terrorism in response to the note verbale by the Secretary-General dated 16 August 1999;

8. *Welcomes* the report of the Secretary-General,[8] and

requests him to continue to seek the views of Member States on the implications of terrorism, in all its forms and manifestations, for the full enjoyment of all human rights and fundamental freedoms, with a view to incorporating them in his report;

9. *Decides* to consider this question at its fifty-sixth session, under the item entitled "Human rights questions".

83rd plenary meeting
17 December 1999

NOTES

1. Resolution 217 A (III).
2. Resolution 2625 (XXV), annex.
3. Resolution 2200 A (XXI), annex.
4. See resolution 50/6.
5. A/CONF.157/24 (Part I), chap. III.
6. See *Official Records of the Economic and Social Council, 1999, Supplement* No. 3 (E/1999/23), chap. II, sect. A.
7. Formerly known as the Subcommission on Prevention of Discrimination and Protection of Minorities.
8. A/54/439.

16

Resolution Adopted by the General Assembly (2 February 2000)

[*on the report of the Sixth Committee (A/54/615)*]

54/110. Measures to eliminate international terrorism

The General Assembly,

Guided by the purposes and principles of the Charter of the United Nations,

Recalling all its relevant resolutions, including resolution 49/60 of 9 December 1994, by which it adopted the Declaration on Measures to Eliminate International Terrorism, and resolutions 50/53 of 11 December 1995, 51/210 of 17 December 1996, 52/165 of 15 December 1997 and 53/108 of 8 December 1998, as well as Security Council resolution 1269 (1999) of 19 October 1999,

Recalling also the Declaration on the Occasion of the Fiftieth Anniversary of the United Nations,[1]

Deeply disturbed by the persistence of terrorist acts, which have been carried out worldwide,

Stressing the need to strengthen further international cooperation between States and between international organizations and agencies, regional organizations and arrangements and the United Nations in order to prevent, combat and eliminate terrorism in all its forms and manifestations, wherever and by whomsoever committed,

Mindful of the need to enhance the role of the United Nations and the relevant specialized agencies in combating international terrorism, and of the proposals of the Secretary-General to enhance the role of the Organization in this respect,

Convinced of the importance of the consideration of measures to eliminate international terrorism by the General Assembly as the universal organ having competence to do so,

Recalling the Declaration on Measures to Eliminate International Terrorism, contained in the annex to resolution 49/60, wherein the General Assembly encouraged States to review urgently the scope of the existing international legal provisions on the prevention, repression and elimination of terrorism in all its forms and manifestations, with the aim of ensuring that there was a comprehensive legal framework covering all aspects of the matter,

Taking note of the final communiqué of the meeting of Ministers for Foreign Affairs and Heads of Delegation of the Movement of Non-Aligned Countries, held in New York on 23 September 1999,[2] which reiterated the collective position of the Movement of Non-Aligned Countries on terrorism and reaffirmed the previous initiative of the Twelfth Conference of Heads of State or Government of Non-Aligned Countries, held at Durban, South Africa, from 29 August to 3 September 1998, calling for an international summit conference under the auspices of the United Nations to formulate a joint organized response of the international community to terrorism in all its forms and manifestations,[3]

Recalling its decision in resolution 53/108 to address at its fifty-fourth session the question of convening a high-level conference in 2000 under the auspices of the United Nations to formulate a joint organized response of the international community to terrorism in all its forms and manifestations,

Noting regional efforts to prevent, combat and eliminate terrorism in all its forms and manifestations, wherever and by whomsoever committed, including through the elaboration of and adherence to regional conventions,

Having examined the report of the Secretary-General,[4]

1. *Strongly condemns* all acts, methods and practices of terrorism as criminal and unjustifiable, wherever and by whomsoever committed;

2. *Reiterates* that criminal acts intended or calculated to provoke a state of terror in the general public, a group of persons or particular persons for political purposes are in any circumstances unjustifiable, whatever the considerations of a political, philosophical, ideological, racial, ethnic, religious or other nature that may be invoked to justify them;

3. *Reiterates its call* upon all States to adopt further measures in accordance with the relevant provisions of international law, including international standards of human rights, to prevent terrorism and to strengthen international cooperation in combating terrorism and, to that end, to consider in particular the implementation of the measures set out in paragraphs 3 (a) to (f) of resolution 51/210;

4. *Also reiterates its call* upon all States, with the aim of enhancing the efficient implementation of relevant legal instruments, to intensify, as and where appropriate, the exchange of information on facts related to terrorism and, in so doing, to avoid the dissemination of inaccurate or unverified information;

5. *Reiterates its call* upon States to refrain from financing, encouraging, providing training for or otherwise supporting terrorist activities;

6. *Reaffirms* that international cooperation as well as actions by States to combat terrorism should be conducted in conformity with the principles of the Charter of the United Nations, international law and relevant international conventions;

7. *Urges* all States that have not yet done so to consider, as a matter of priority, becoming parties to relevant conventions and protocols as referred to in paragraph 6 of resolution 51/210, as well as the International Convention for the Suppression of Terrorist Bombings,[5] and calls upon all States to enact, as appropriate, domestic legislation necessary to implement the

provisions of those conventions and protocols, to ensure that the jurisdiction of their courts enables them to bring to trial the perpetrators of terrorist acts, and to cooperate with and provide support and assistance to other States and relevant international and regional organizations to that end;

8. *Reaffirms* the Declaration on Measures to Eliminate International Terrorism contained in the annex to resolution 49/60 and the Declaration to Supplement the 1994 Declaration on Measures to Eliminate International Terrorism contained in the annex to resolution 51/210, and calls upon all States to implement them;

9. *Notes* the establishment of the Terrorism Prevention Branch of the Centre for International Crime Prevention in Vienna, and welcomes its efforts, after reviewing existing possibilities within the United Nations system, to enhance through research and technical cooperation the capabilities of the United Nations in the prevention of terrorism;

10. *Invites* States that have not yet done so to submit to the Secretary-General information on their national laws and regulations regarding the prevention and suppression of acts of international terrorism;

11. *Invites* regional intergovernmental organizations to submit to the Secretary-General information on the measures they have adopted at the regional level to eliminate international terrorism;

12. *Decides* that the Ad Hoc Committee established by General Assembly resolution 51/210 of 17 December 1996 shall continue to elaborate a draft international convention for the suppression of acts of nuclear terrorism with a view to completing the instrument, shall address means of further developing a comprehensive legal framework of conventions dealing with international terrorism, including considering the elaboration of a comprehensive convention on international terrorism, and shall address the question of convening a high-level conference under the auspices of the United Nations to

formulate a joint organized response of the international community to terrorism in all its forms and manifestations;

13. *Decides also* that the Ad Hoc Committee shall meet from 14 to 18 February 2000, devoting appropriate time to the consideration of the outstanding issues relating to the elaboration of a draft international convention for the suppression of acts of nuclear terrorism, and that it shall address the question of convening a high-level conference under the auspices of the United Nations to formulate a joint organized response of the international community to terrorism in all its forms and manifestations, and that the work shall continue, including beginning consideration with a view to the elaboration of a comprehensive convention on international terrorism within a comprehensive legal framework of conventions dealing with international terrorism, during the fifty-fifth session of the General Assembly from 25 September to 6 October 2000, within the framework of a working group of the Sixth Committee, and that the Ad Hoc Committee shall be convened in 2001 to continue its work;

14. *Requests* the Secretary-General to continue to provide the Ad Hoc Committee with the necessary facilities for the performance of its work;

15. *Requests* the Ad Hoc Committee to report to the General Assembly at its fifty-fourth session in the event of the completion of the draft international convention for the suppression of acts of nuclear terrorism;

16. *Also requests* the Ad Hoc Committee to report to the General Assembly at its fifty-fifth session on progress made in the implementation of its mandate;

17. *Decides* to include in the provisional agenda of its fifty-fifth session the item entitled "Measures to eliminate international terrorism".

76th plenary meeting
9 December 1999

NOTES

1. See resolution 50/6.
2. A/54/469-S/1999/1063, annex; see *Official Records of the Security Council, Fifty-fourth Year, Supplement for October, November and December 1999*, document S/1999/1063.
3. See A/53/667-S/1998/1071, annex I, paras. 149-162; see *Official Records of the Security Council, Fifty-third Year, Supplement for October, November and December 1998*, document S/1998/1071.
4. A/54/301 and Add.1.
5. Resolution 52/164, annex.

17

Statement by the President of the Security Council (22 October 1999)

At the 4055th meeting of the Security Council, held on 22 October 1999, in connection with the Council's consideration of the item entitled "The situation in Afghanistan", the President of the Security Council made the following statement on behalf of the Council :

> "The Security Council has considered the report of the Secretary-General concerning the situation in Afghanistan and its implications for international peace and security of 21 September 1999 (A/54/378-S/1999/994).
>
> "The Security Council reiterates its grave concern at the continued Afghan conflict, which is a serious and growing threat to regional and international peace and security. It strongly condemns the Taliban for the launching in July 1999, only one week after the meeting of the 'Six plus Two' group in Tashkent, of a new offensive, despite the repeated demands by the Council to cease fighting. This has undermined international efforts to facilitate the restoration of peace in Afghanistan. The fighting following the offensive has resulted in enormous suffering to the civilian population of Afghanistan. The Taliban has a primary responsibility for this.

"The Security Council reiterates that there is no military solution to the conflict in Afghanistan and that only a negotiated political settlement aimed at the establishment of a broad-based, multi-ethnic and fully representative government acceptable to all Afghans can lead to peace and reconciliation. It recalls its demand that the parties to the conflict, especially the Taliban, resume negotiations under United Nations auspices without delay and preconditions in full compliance with the relevant resolutions of the General Assembly and the Council. The Council notes that the United Front of Afghanistan have repeatedly made clear that they are willing to talk with the Taliban in order to reach a solution to the country's problems.

"The Security Council reiterates that outside interference in the internal affairs of Afghanistan, including the involvement of foreign combatants and military personnel and the supply of weapons and other materials used in the conflict, should cease immediately. It calls upon all States to take resolute measures to prohibit their military personnel from planning and participating in combat operations in Afghanistan, and immediately to withdraw their personnel and to assure that the supply of ammunition and other war-making materials is halted. The Council expresses its deep distress over reports indicating the involvement in the fighting in Afghanistan, on the side of the Taliban forces, of thousands of non-Afghans nationals, mostly from religious schools and some of whom are below the age of 14.

"The Security Council reaffirms its full support for the efforts of the United Nations, in particular the activities of the United Nations Special Mission to Afghanistan (UNSMA) and those of the Special Envoy of the Secretary-General for Afghanistan, in facilitating the political process towards the goals of national reconciliation and a lasting political settlement with the participation of all parties to the conflict and all segments of Afghan society, and reiterates its position that the United Nations must continue to play its central and impartial role in international efforts towards a peaceful resolution of the Afghan conflict.

"The Security Council expresses its grave concern at the seriously deteriorating humanitarian situation in Afghanistan. It calls upon all Afghan parties, and in particular the Taliban, to take the necessary steps to secure the uninterrupted supply of humanitarian aid to all in need of it and in this connection not to create impediments to the activities of the United Nations humanitarian agencies and international humanitarian organizations.

"The Security Council once again urges all Afghan factions to cooperate fully with UNSMA and international humanitarian organizations, and calls upon them, in particular the Taliban, to take the necessary steps to ensure the safety and freedom of movement of such personnel.

"The Security Council welcomes the Declaration on Fundamental Principles for a Peaceful Settlement of the Conflict in Afghanistan (A/54/174-S/1999/812, annex) adopted by the >Six plus Two= group on 19 July 1999 in Tashkent, particularly the agreement of members of the group not to provide military support to any Afghan party and to prevent the use of their territories for such purposes. It urges the members of the group and the Afghan factions to implement these principles in support of the efforts of the United Nations towards a peaceful resolution of the Afghan conflict.

"The Security Council strongly condemns the continuing use of Afghan territory, especially areas controlled by the Taliban, for the sheltering and training of terrorists and planning of terrorist acts, and reaffirms its conviction that the suppression of international terrorism is essential for the maintenance of international peace and security. It insists that the Taliban cease the provision of sanctuary and training for international terrorists and their organizations, take effective measures to ensure that the territory under its control is not used for terrorist installations and camps or for the preparation or organization of terrorist acts against other States or their citizens, and cooperate with efforts to bring indicted terrorists to justice. The Council demands once again that the Taliban turn over indicted terrorist Usama bin Laden to appropriate authorities as set out in its resolution 1267 (1999) of 15 October 1999. It reaffirms its decision to implement on 14 November 1999 the measures contained in that resolution, unless the Secretary-General reports that the Taliban has fully complied with the obligation set out in paragraph 2 of that resolution.

"The Security Council is deeply disturbed also by a significant increase in the cultivation, production and trafficking of drugs in Afghanistan, especially in areas controlled by the Taliban, which will contribute to the war-making capabilities of the Afghans and will have even more serious international consequences. It demands that the Taliban, as well as others, halt all illegal drug activities. The Council calls upon Member States, in particular those neighbouring Afghanistan, and all others concerned to undertake concerted measures to stop the trafficking of illegal drugs from Afghanistan.

"The Security Council deplores the worsening human rights situation in Afghanistan. It expresses particular alarm at the continuing disregard by the Taliban of the concerns expressed by the international community. The Council underlines the unacceptability of the forced displacement of the civilian population, in particular that conducted by the Taliban during their recent offensive, summary executions, the deliberate abuse and arbitrary detentions of civilians, violence and continuing discrimination against women and girls, the separation of men from their families, the use of child soldiers, the widespread burning of crops and destruction of homes, the indiscriminate bombing and other violations of human rights and international humanitarian law in Afghanistan. It calls upon all Afghan parties, especially the Taliban, to put an end to such practices, to adhere to the international norms and standards in this sphere, to take urgent measures to improve the human rights situation and, as an immediate first step, to ensure the protection of civilians.

"The Security Council reiterates that the capture by the Taliban of the Consulate-General of the Islamic Republic of Iran and the murder of the Iranian diplomats and a journalist in Mazar-e-Sharif constitute flagrant violations of international law. It demands that the Taliban cooperate fully with the United Nations in investigating these crimes with a view to prosecuting those responsible.

"The Security Council looks forward to the Secretary-General's next report on the situation in Afghanistan, and encourages him to review options for the Security Council and the General Assembly.

"The Security Council deplores the failure of the leadership of the Taliban to take measures to comply with the demands made in its previous resolutions, especially to conclude a ceasefire and to resume negotiations, and in this context reaffirms its readiness to consider the imposition of measures, in accordance with its responsibility under the Charter of the United Nations, with the aim of achieving the full implementation of its relevant resolutions."

18

Resolution 1269 (1999) Adopted by the Security Council at its 4053rd meeting on 19 October 1999

The Security Council,

Deeply concerned by the increase in acts of international terrorism which endangers the lives and well-being of individuals worldwide as well as the peace and security of all States,

Condemning all acts of terrorism, irrespective of motive, wherever and by whomever committed,

Mindful of all relevant resolutions of the General Assembly, including resolution 49/60 of 9 December 1994, by which it adopted the Declaration on Measures to Eliminate International Terrorism,

Emphasizing the necessity to intensify the fight against terrorism at the national level and to strengthen, under the auspices of the United Nations, effective international cooperation in this field on the basis of the principles of the Charter of the United Nations and norms of international law, including respect for international humanitarian law and human rights,

Supporting the efforts to promote universal participation in and implementation of the existing international anti-terrorist conventions, as well as to develop new international instruments to counter the terrorist threat,

Commending the work done by the General Assembly,

relevant United Nations organs and specialized agencies and regional and other organizations to combat international terrorism,

Determined to contribute, in accordance with the Charter of the United Nations, to the efforts to combat terrorism in all its forms,

Reaffirming that the suppression of acts of international terrorism, including those in which States are involved, is an essential contribution to the maintenance of international peace and security,

1. *Unequivocally condemns* all acts, methods and practices of terrorism as criminal and unjustifiable, regardless of their motivation, in all their forms and manifestations, wherever and by whomever committed, in particular those which could threaten international peace and security;

2. *Calls upon* all States to implement fully the international anti-terrorist conventions to which they are parties, *encourages* all States to consider as a matter of priority adhering to those to which they are not parties, and *encourages also* the speedy adoption of the pending conventions;

3. *Stresses* the vital role of the United Nations in strengthening international cooperation in combating terrorism and, *emphasizes* the importance of enhanced coordination among States, international and regional organizations;

4. *Calls upon* all States to take, *inter alia*, in the context of such cooperation and coordination, appropriate steps to :

- cooperate with each other, particularly through bilateral and multilateral agreements and arrangements, to prevent and suppress terrorist acts, protect their nationals and other persons against terrorist attacks and bring to justice the perpetrators of such acts;
- prevent and suppress in their territories through all lawful means the preparation and financing of any acts of terrorism;
- deny those who plan, finance or commit terrorist acts

safe havens by ensuring their apprehension and prosecution or extradition;

- take appropriate measures in conformity with the relevant provisions of national and international law, including international standards of human rights, before granting refugee status, for the purpose of ensuring that the asylum-seeker has not participated in terrorist acts;
- exchange information in accordance with international and domestic law, and cooperate on administrative and judicial matters in order to prevent the commission of terrorist acts;

5. *Requests* the Secretary-General, in his reports to the General Assembly, in particular submitted in accordance with its resolution 50/53 on measures to eliminate international terrorism, to pay special attention to the need to prevent and fight the threat to international peace and security as a result of terrorist activities;

6. *Expresses* its readiness to consider relevant provisions of the reports mentioned in paragraph 5 above and to take necessary steps in accordance with its responsibilities under the Charter of the United Nations in order to counter terrorist threats to international peace and security;

7. *Decides* to remain seized of this matter.

19

UN Security Council Resolution on International Terrorism (document S/1999/1071), 18 October 1999

"The Security Council,

"Deeply concerned by the increase in acts of international terrorism which endangers the lives and well-being of individuals worldwide as well as the peace and security of all States,

"Condemning all acts of terrorism, irrespective of motive, wherever and by whomever committed,

"Mindful of all relevant resolutions of the General Assembly, including resolution 49/60 of December 9, 1994, by which it adopted Declaration on Measures to Eliminate International Terrorism,

"Emphasizing the necessity to intensify the fight against terrorism at the national level and to strengthen, under the auspices of the United Nations, effective international cooperation in this field on the basis of the principles of the Charter of the United Nations and norms of international law, including respect for international humanitarian law and human rights,

"Supporting the efforts to promote universal participation in and implementation of the existing international anti-terrorist conventions, as well as to develop new international instruments to counter the terrorist threat,

"Commending the work done by the General Assembly,

relevant United Nations organs and specialized agencies and regional and other organizations, to combat international terrorism,

"Determined to contribute, in accordance with the Charter of the United Nations, to the efforts to combat terrorism in all its forms,

"Reaffirming that the suppression of acts of international terrorism, including those in which States are involved, is an essential contribution to the maintenance of international peace and security,

"1. Unequivocally condemns all acts, methods and practices of terrorism as criminal and unjustifiable, regardless of their motivation, in all their forms and manifestations, wherever and by whomever committed, in particular those which could threaten international peace and security;

"2. Calls upon all States to implement fully the international anti-terrorist conventions to which they are parties, encourages all States to consider as a matter of priority adhering to those to which they are not parties; and encourages also the speedy adoption of the pending conventions;

"3. Stresses the vital role of the United Nations in strengthening international cooperation in combating terrorism and emphasizes the importance of enhanced coordination among States, international and regional organizations;

"4. Calls upon all States to take, inter alia, in the context of such cooperation and coordination, appropriate steps to :

- cooperate with each other, particularly through bilateral and multilateral agreements and arrangements, to prevent and suppress terrorist acts, protect their nationals and other persons against terrorist attacks and bring to justice the perpetrators of such acts;
- prevent and suppress in their territories through all lawful means the preparation and financing of any acts of terrorism;
- deny those who plan, finance or commit terrorist acts

safe havens by ensuring their apprehension and prosecution or extradition;

- take appropriate measures in conformity with the relevant provisions of national and international law, including international standards of human rights, before granting refugee status, for the purpose of ensuring that the asylum-seeker has not participated in terrorist acts;
- exchange information in accordance with international and domestic law, and cooperate on administrative and judicial matters in order to prevent the commission of terrorist acts;

"5. Requests the Secretary-General, in his reports to the General Assembly, in particular submitted in accordance with its resolution 50/53 on measures to eliminate international terrorism, to pay special attention to the need to prevent and fight the threat to international peace and security as a result of terrorist activities;

"6. Expresses its readiness to consider relevant provisions of the reports mentioned in paragraph 5 above and to take necessary steps in accordance with its responsibilities under the Charter of the United Nations in order to counter terrorist threats to international peace and security;

"7. Decides to remain seized of this matter."

20

Resolution 1267 (1999) Adopted by the Security Council at its 4051st meeting on 15 October 1999

The Security Council,

Reaffirming its previous resolutions, in particular resolutions 1189 (1998) of 13 August 1998, 1193 (1998) of 28 August 1998 and 1214 (1998) of 8 December 1998, and the statements of its President on the situation in Afghanistan,

Reaffirming its strong commitment to the sovereignty, independence, territorial integrity and national unity of Afghanistan, and its respect for Afghanistan's cultural and historical heritage,

Reiterating its deep concern over the continuing violations of international humanitarian law and of human rights, particularly discrimination against women and girls, and over the significant rise in the illicit production of opium, and stressing that the capture by the Taliban of the Consulate-General of the Islamic Republic of Iran and the murder of Iranian diplomats and a journalist in Mazar-e-Sharif constituted flagrant violations of established international law,

Recalling the relevant international counter-terrorism conventions and in particular the obligations of parties to those conventions to extradite or prosecute terrorists,

Strongly condemning the continuing use of Afghan territory, especially areas controlled by the Taliban, for the sheltering and training of terrorists and planning of terrorist acts, and *reaffirming* its conviction that the suppression of international terrorism is essential for the maintenance of international peace and security,

Deploring the fact that the Taliban continues to provide safe haven to Usama bin Laden and to allow him and others associated with him to operate a network of terrorist training camps from Taliban-controlled territory and to use Afghanistan as a base from which to sponsor international terrorist operations,

Noting the indictment of Usama bin Laden and his associates by the United States of America for, *inter alia*, the 7 August 1998 bombings of the United States embassies in Nairobi, Kenya, and Dar es Salaam, Tanzania and for conspiring to kill American nationals outside the United States, and noting also the request of the United States of America to the Taliban to surrender them for trial (S/1999/1021),

Determining that the failure of the Taliban authorities to respond to the demands in paragraph 13 of resolution 1214 (1998) constitutes a threat to international peace and security,

Stressing its determination to ensure respect for its resolutions,

Acting under Chapter VII of the Charter of the United Nations,

1. *Insists* that the Afghan faction known as the Taliban, which also calls itself the Islamic Emirate of Afghanistan, comply promptly with its previous resolutions and in particular cease the provision of sanctuary and training for international terrorists and their organizations, take appropriate effective measures to ensure that the territory under its control is not used for terrorist installations and camps, or for the preparation or organization of terrorist acts against other States or their citizens, and cooperate with efforts to bring indicted terrorists to justice;

2. *Demands* that the Taliban turn over Usama bin Laden without further delay to appropriate authorities in a country

where he has been indicted, or to appropriate authorities in a country where he will be returned to such a country, or to appropriate authorities in a country where he will be arrested and effectively brought to justice;

3. *Decides* that on 14 November 1999 all States shall impose the measures set out in paragraph 4 below, unless the Council has previously decided, on the basis of a report of the Secretary-General, that the Taliban has fully complied with the obligation set out in paragraph 2 above;

4. *Decides further* that, in order to enforce paragraph 2 above, all States shall :

(a) Deny permission for any aircraft to take off from or land in their territory if it is owned, leased or operated by or on behalf of the Taliban as designated by the Committee established by paragraph 6 below, unless the particular flight has been approved in advance by the Committee on the grounds of humanitarian need, including religious obligation such as the performance of the Hajj;

(b) Freeze funds and other financial resources, including funds derived or generated from property owned or controlled directly or indirectly by the Taliban, or by any undertaking owned or controlled by the Taliban, as designated by the Committee established by paragraph 6 below, and ensure that neither they nor any other funds or financial resources so designated are made available, by their nationals or by any persons within their territory, to or for the benefit of the Taliban or any undertaking owned or controlled, directly or indirectly, by the Taliban, except as may be authorized by the Committee on a case-by-case basis on the grounds of humanitarian need;

5. *Urges* all States to cooperate with efforts to fulfil the demand in paragraph 2 above, and to consider further measures against Usama bin Laden and his associates;

6. *Decides* to establish, in accordance with rule 28 of its provisional rules of procedure, a Committee of the Security Council consisting of all the members of the Council to undertake the following tasks and to report on its work to the Council with its observations and recommendations :

(a) To seek from all States further information regarding the action taken by them with a view to effectively implementing the measures imposed by paragraph 4 above;

(b) To consider information brought to its attention by States concerning violations of the measures imposed by paragraph 4 above and to recommend appropriate measures in response thereto;

(c) To make periodic reports to the Council on the impact, including the humanitarian implications, of the measures imposed by paragraph 4 above;

(d) To make periodic reports to the Council on information submitted to it regarding alleged violations of the measures imposed by paragraph 4 above, identifying where possible persons or entities reported to be engaged in such violations;

(e) To designate the aircraft and funds or other financial resources referred to in paragraph 4 above in order to facilitate the implementation of the measures imposed by that paragraph;

(f) To consider requests for exemptions from the measures imposed by paragraph 4 above as provided in that paragraph, and to decide on the granting of an exemption to these measures in respect of the payment by the International Air Transport Association (IATA) to the aeronautical authority of Afghanistan on behalf of international airlines for air traffic control services;

(g) To examine the reports submitted pursuant to paragraph 9 below;

7. *Calls upon* all States to act strictly in accordance with

the provisions of this resolution, notwithstanding the existence of any rights or obligations conferred or imposed by any international agreement or any contract entered into or any licence or permit granted prior to the date of coming into force of the measures imposed by paragraph 4 above;

8. *Calls upon* States to bring proceedings against persons and entities within their jurisdiction that violate the measures imposed by paragraph 4 above and to impose appropriate penalties;

9. *Calls upon* all States to cooperate fully with the Committee established by paragraph 6 above in the fulfilment of its tasks, including supplying such information as may be required by the Committee in pursuance of this resolution;

10. *Requests* all States to report to the Committee established by paragraph 6 above within 30 days of the coming into force of the measures imposed by paragraph 4 above on the steps they have taken with a view to effectively implementing paragraph 4 above;

11. *Requests* the Secretary-General to provide all necessary assistance to the Committee established by paragraph 6 above and to make the necessary arrangements in the Secretariat for this purpose;

12. *Requests* the Committee established by paragraph 6 above to determine appropriate arrangements, on the basis of recommendations of the Secretariat, with competent international organizations, neighbouring and other States, and parties concerned with a view to improving the monitoring of the implementation of the measures imposed by paragraph 4 above;

13. *Requests* the Secretariat to submit for consideration by the Committee established by paragraph 6 above information received from Governments and public sources on possible violations of the measures imposed by paragraph 4 above;

14. *Decides* to terminate the measures imposed by paragraph 4 above once the Secretary-General reports to the Security

Council that the Taliban has fulfilled the obligation set out in paragraph 2 above;

15. *Expresses* its readiness to consider the imposition of further measures, in accordance with its responsibility under the Charter of the United Nations, with the aim of achieving the full implementation of this resolution;

16. *Decides* to remain actively seized of the matter.

21

UN Security Council Adopts Limited Sanctions Against Taliban (15 October 1999)

Canada, the Netherlands, Russian Federation, Slovenia, United Kingdom of Great Britain and Northern Ireland and United States of America : draft resolution

The Security Council,

Reaffirming its previous resolutions, in particular resolutions 1189 (1998) of 13 August 1998, 1193 (1998) of 28 August 1998 and 1214 (1998) of 8 December 1998, and the statements of its President on the situation in Afghanistan,

Reaffirming its strong commitment to the sovereignty, independence, territorial integrity and national unity of Afghanistan, and its respect for Afghanistan's cultural and historical heritage,

Reiterating its deep concern over the continuing violations of international humanitarian law and of human rights, particularly discrimination against women and girls, and over the significant rise in the illicit production of opium, and stressing that the capture by the Taliban of the Consulate-General of the Islamic Republic of Iran and the murder of Iranian diplomats and a journalist in Mazar-e-Sharif constituted flagrant violations of established international law,

Recalling the relevant international counter-terrorism

conventions and in particular the obligations of parties to those conventions to extradite or prosecute terrorists,

Strongly condemning the continuing use of Afghan territory, especially areas controlled by the Taliban, for the sheltering and training of terrorists and planning of terrorist acts, and reaffirming its conviction that the suppression of international terrorism is essential for the maintenance of international peace and security,

Deploring the fact that the Taliban continues to provide safe haven to Usama bin Laden and to allow him and others associated with him to operate a network of terrorist training camps from Taliban-controlled territory and to use Afghanistan as a base from which to sponsor international terrorist operations,

Noting the indictment of Usama bin Laden and his associates by the United states of America for, inter alia, the 7 August 1996 bombings of the United States embassies in Nairobi, Kenya, and Dar es Salaam, Tanzania and for conspiring to kill American nationals outside the United States, and noting also the request of the United States of America to the Taliban to surrender them for trial (S/1999/1021),

Determining that the failure of the Taliban authorities to respond to the demands in paragraph 13 of resolution 1214 (1998) constitutes a threat to international peace and security,

Stressing its determination to ensure respect for its resolutions,

Acting under Chapter VII of the Charter of the United Nations,

1. Insists that the Afghan faction known as the Taliban, which also calls itself the Islamic Emirate of Afghanistan, comply promptly with its previous resolutions and in particular cease the provision of sanctuary and training for international terrorists and their organizations, take appropriate effective measures to ensure that the territory under its control is not used for terrorist installations and camps, or for the preparation or organization of terrorist acts against

other States or their citizens, and cooperate with efforts to bring indicted terrorists to justice;

2. Demands that the Taliban turn over Usama bin Laden without further delay to appropriate authorities in a country where he has been indicted, or to appropriate authorities in a country where he will be returned to such a country, or to appropriate authorities in a country where he will be arrested and effectively brought to justice;

3. Decides that on 14 November 1999 all States shall impose the measures set out in paragraph 4 below, unless the Council has previously decided, on the basis of a report of the Secretary-General, that the Taliban has fully complied with the obligation set out in paragraph 2 above;

4. Decides further that, in order to enforce paragraph 2 above, all States shall :

   (a) Deny permission for any aircraft to take off from or land in their territory if it is owned, leased or operated by or on behalf of the Taliban as designated by the Committee established by paragraph 6 below, unless the particular flight has been approved in advance by the Committee on the grounds of humanitarian need, including religious obligation such as the performance of the Hajj;

   (b) Freeze funds and other financial resources, including funds derived or generated from property owned or controlled directly or indirectly by the Taliban, or by any undertaking owned or controlled by the Taliban, as designated by the Committee established by paragraph 6 below, and ensure that neither they nor any other funds or financial resources so designated are made available, by their nationals or by any persons within their territory, to or for the benefit of the Taliban or any undertaking owned or controlled, directly or indirectly, by the Taliban, except as may be authorized by the Committee on a case-by-case basis on the grounds of humanitarian need;

5. Urges all States to cooperate with efforts to fulfil the demand in paragraph 2 above, and to consider further measures against Usama bin Laden and his associates;
6. Decides to establish, in accordance with rule 28 of its provisional rules of procedure, a Committee of the Security Council consisting of all the members of the Council to undertake the following tasks and to report on its work to the Council with its observations and recommendations :
   (a) To seek from all States further information regarding the action taken by them with a view to effectively implementing the measures imposed by paragraph 4 above;
   (b) To consider information brought to its attention by States concerning violations of the measures imposed by paragraph 4 above and to recommend appropriate measures in response thereto;
   (c) To make periodic reports to the Council an the impact, including the humanitarian implications, of the measures imposed by paragraph 4 above;
   (d) To make periodic reports to the Council on information submitted to it regarding alleged violations of the measures imposed by paragraph 4 above, identifying where possible persons or entities reported to be engaged in such violations;
   (e) To designate the aircraft and funds or other financial resources referred to in paragraph 4 above in order to facilitate the implementation of the measures imposed by that paragraph;
   (f) To consider requests for exemptions from the measures imposed by paragraph 4 above as provided

in that paragraph, and to decide on the granting of an exemption to these measures in respect of the payment by the International Air Transport Association (IATA) to the aeronautical authority of Afghanistan on behalf of international airlines for air traffic control services;

(g) To examine the reports submitted pursuant to paragraph 9 below;

7. Calls upon all States to act strictly in accordance with the provisions of this resolution, notwithstanding the existence of any rights or obligations conferred or imposed by any international agreement or any contract entered into or any licence or permit granted prior to the date of coming into force of the measures imposed by paragraph 4 above;

8. Calls upon States to bring proceedings against persons and entities within their jurisdiction that violate the measures imposed by paragraph 4 above and to impose appropriate penalties;

9. Calls upon all States to cooperate fully with the Committee established by paragraph 6 above in the fulfillment of its tasks, including supplying such information as may be required by the Committee in pursuance of this resolution;

10. Requests all States to report to the Committee established by paragraph 6 above within 30 days of the coming into force of the measures imposed by paragraph 4 above on the steps they have taken with a view to effectively implementing paragraph 4 above;

11. Requests the Secretary-General to provide all necessary assistance to the Committee established by paragraph 6 above and to make the necessary arrangements in the Secretariat for this purpose;

12. Requests the Committee established by paragraph 6 above to determine appropriate arrangements, on the

basis of recommendations of the Secretariat, with competent international organizations, neighbouring and other States, and parties concerned with a view to improving the monitoring of the implementation of the measures imposed by paragraph 4 above;

13. Requests the Secretariat to submit for consideration by the Committee established by paragraph 6 above information received from Governments and public sources on possible violations of the measures imposed by paragraph 4 above;

14. Decides to terminate the measures imposed by paragraph 4 above once the Secretary-General reports to the Security Council that the Taliban has fulfilled the obligation set out in paragraph 2 above;

15. Expresses its readiness to consider the imposition of further measures, in accordance with its responsibility under the Charter of the United Nations, with the aim of achieving the full implementation of this resolution;

16. Decides to remain actively seized of the matter.

22

Resolution Adopted by the General Assembly (26 January 1999)

[*on the report of the Sixth Committee (A/53/636)*]

53/108. Measures to eliminate international terrorism

The General Assembly,

Guided by the purposes and principles of the Charter of the United Nations,

Recalling all its relevant resolutions, including resolution 49/60 of 9 December 1994, by which it adopted the Declaration on Measures to Eliminate International Terrorism, and resolutions 50/53 of 11 December 1995, 51/210 of 17 December 1996 and 52/165 of 15 December 1997,

Recalling also the Declaration on the Occasion of the Fiftieth Anniversary of the United Nations,[1]

Deeply disturbed by the persistence of terrorist acts, which have been carried out worldwide,

Stressing the need to strengthen further international cooperation between States and between international organizations and agencies, regional organizations and arrangements and the United Nations in order to prevent, combat and eliminate terrorism in all its forms and manifestations, wherever and by whomsoever committed,

Mindful of the need to enhance the role of the United

Nations and the relevant specialized agencies in combating international terrorism, and of the proposals of the Secretary-General to enhance the role of the Organization in this respect,

Recalling that in the Declaration on Measures to Eliminate International Terrorism, contained in the annex to resolution 49/60, the General Assembly encouraged States to review urgently the scope of the existing international legal provisions on the prevention, repression and elimination of terrorism in all its forms and manifestations, with the aim of ensuring that there was a comprehensive legal framework covering all aspects of the matter,

Bearing in mind the possibility of considering in the near future the elaboration of a comprehensive convention on international terrorism,

Bearing in mind also that the Twelfth Conference of Heads of State or Government of Non-Aligned Countries, held at Durban, South Africa, from 29 August to 3 September 1998, reaffirmed its collective position on terrorism and as a recent initiative called for an international summit conference under the auspices of the United Nations to formulate a joint organized response of the international community to terrorism in all its forms and manifestations,[2]

Recognizing the urgent need to enhance international cooperation to prevent terrorist financing and to develop an appropriate legal instrument,

Having examined the report of the Secretary-General,[3]

1. *Strongly condemns* all acts, methods and practices of terrorism as criminal and unjustifiable, wherever and by whomsoever committed;

2. *Reiterates* that criminal acts intended or calculated to provoke a state of terror in the general public, a group of persons or particular persons for political purposes are in any circumstances unjustifiable, whatever the considerations of a political, philosophical, ideological, racial, ethnic, religious or other nature that may be invoked to justify them;

3. *Reiterates its call* upon all States to adopt further measures in accordance with the relevant provisions of international law, including international standards of human rights, to prevent terrorism and to strengthen international cooperation in combating terrorism and, to that end, to consider in particular the implementation of the measures set out in paragraphs 3 (a) to (f) of its resolution 51/210;

4. *Also reiterates its call* upon all States, with the aim of enhancing the efficient implementation of relevant legal instruments, to intensify, as and where appropriate, the exchange of information on facts related to terrorism and, in so doing, to avoid the dissemination of inaccurate or unverified information;

5. *Reiterates its call* upon States to refrain from financing, encouraging, providing training for or otherwise supporting terrorist activities;

6. *Reaffirms* that international cooperation as well as actions by States to combat terrorism should be conducted in conformity with the principles of the Charter of the United Nations, international law and relevant international conventions;

7. *Urges* all States that have not yet done so to consider, as a matter of priority, becoming parties to relevant conventions and protocols as referred to in paragraph 6 of resolution 51/210, as well as the International Convention for the Suppression of Terrorist Bombings, and calls upon all States to enact, as appropriate,[4] domestic legislation necessary to implement the provisions of those conventions and protocols, to ensure that the jurisdiction of their courts enables them to bring to trial the perpetrators of terrorist acts, and to cooperate with and provide support and assistance to other States and relevant international and regional organizations to that end;

8. *Reaffirms* the Declaration on Measures to Eliminate International Terrorism contained in the annex to resolution 49/60 and the Declaration to Supplement the 1994 Declaration on Measures to Eliminate International Terrorism contained in the annex to resolution 51/210, and calls upon all States to implement them;

9. *Takes note* of the measures aimed at strengthening the capacity of the Centre for International Crime Prevention of the Secretariat to enhance international cooperation and improve the response of Governments to terrorism in all its forms and manifestations;

10. *Decides* to address at its fifty-fourth session the question of convening a high-level conference in 2000 under the auspices of the United Nations to formulate a joint organized response of the international community to terrorism in all its forms and manifestations;

11. *Decides also* that the Ad Hoc Committee established by General Assembly resolution 51/210 of 17 December 1996 shall continue to elaborate a draft international convention for the suppression of acts of nuclear terrorism with a view to completing the instrument, shall elaborate a draft international convention for the suppression of terrorist financing to supplement related existing international instruments, and subsequently shall address means of further developing a comprehensive legal framework of conventions dealing with international terrorism, including considering, on a priority basis, the elaboration of a comprehensive convention on international terrorism;

12. *Decides further* that the Ad Hoc Committee shall meet from 15 to 26 March 1999, devoting appropriate time to the consideration of the outstanding issues relating to the elaboration of a draft international convention for the suppression of acts of nuclear terrorism, and that it shall initiate the elaboration of a draft international convention for the suppression of terrorist financing, and recommends that the work continue during the fifty-fourth session of the General Assembly from 27 September to 8 October 1999, within the framework of a working group of the Sixth Committee, and that the Ad Hoc Committee be convened in 2000 to continuc its work as referred to in paragraph 11 above;

13. *Requests* the Secretary-General to continue to provide

the Ad Hoc Committee with the necessary facilities for the performance of its work;

14. *Requests* the Ad Hoc Committee to report to the General Assembly at its fifty-third session in the event of the completion of the draft convention for the suppression of acts of nuclear terrorism;

15. *Also requests* the Ad Hoc Committee to report to the General Assembly at its fifty-fourth session on progress made in the implementation of its mandate;

16. *Decides* to include in the provisional agenda of its fifty-fourth session the item entitled "Measures to eliminate international terrorism".

83rd plenary meeting
8 December 1998

NOTES

1. See resolution 50/6.
2. See A/53/667–S/1998/1071, annex I, paras. 149-162; see *Official Records of the Security Council, Fifty-third Year, Supplement for October, November and December 1998,* document S/1998/1071.
3. A/53/314 and Corr.2 and Add.1.
4. Resolution 52/164, annex.

23

Resolution 1214 (1998) Adopted by the Security Council at its 3952nd meeting on 8 December 1998

The Security Council,

Having considered the situation in Afghanistan,

Reaffirming its previous resolutions, in particular resolutions 1189 (1998) of 13 August 1998 and 1193 (1998) of 28 August 1998, and the statements of its President on the situation in Afghanistan,

Recalling resolution 52/211 of the General Assembly,

Expressing its grave concern at the continued Afghan conflict, which has recently sharply escalated as a result of the offensive by the Taliban forces, which is continuing despite the repeated pleas by the Security Council to cease the fighting, and causing a serious and growing threat to regional and international peace and security, as well as extensive human suffering, further destruction, refugee flows and other forcible displacement of large numbers of people,

Deploring the fact that despite the readiness of the United Front of Afghanistan to conclude a durable ceasefire and to enter into a political dialogue with the Taliban, fighting continues on both sides,

Concerned also by the increasingly ethnic nature of the conflict, by reports of ethnic and religious-based persecution, particularly against the Shiites, and by the threat this poses to the unity of the Afghan State,

Reaffirming its strong commitment to the sovereignty, independence, territorial integrity and national unity of Afghanistan, and its respect for its cultural and historical heritage,

Reiterating that any outside interference in the internal affairs of Afghanistan, including the involvement of foreign military personnel and the supply of arms and ammunition to all parties to the conflict, should cease immediately,

Reaffirming its full support for the efforts of the United Nations, in particular the activities of the United Nations Special Mission to Afghanistan (UNSMA) and those of the Special Envoy of the Secretary-General for Afghanistan in facilitating the political process towards the goals of national reconciliation and a lasting political settlement with the participation of all parties to the conflict and all segments of Afghan society, and reiterating its position that the United Nations must continue to play its central and impartial role in international efforts towards a peaceful resolution of the Afghan conflict,

Welcoming the work of the "six plus two" group, and supporting in this regard the "points of common understanding" (A/53/455-S/1998/913, annex) adopted at its meeting, at the level of Foreign Ministers, convened and chaired by the Secretary-General on 21 September 1998,

Deeply concerned at the serious and rapidly deteriorating humanitarian crisis in Afghanistan, deploring in this regard the measures taken by the Taliban which resulted in the evacuation of the United Nations humanitarian personnel from Afghanistan and underlining the urgent need for the prompt implementation of the necessary security requirements to allow their early return,

Reaffirming that all parties to the conflict are bound to comply with their obligations under international humanitarian law and in particular under the Geneva Conventions of 12 August 1949, and that persons who commit or order the commission of breaches of the Conventions are individually responsible in respect of such breaches,

Deeply disturbed by the continuing use of Afghan territory, especially areas controlled by the Taliban, for the sheltering and training of terrorists and the planning of terrorist acts, and reiterating that the suppression of international terrorism is essential for the maintenance of international peace and security,

Deeply disturbed also by the growing cultivation, production and trafficking of drugs in Afghanistan, especially in areas controlled by the Taliban,

Reiterating its deep concern at the continuing discrimination against girls and women and at other violations of human rights and of international humanitarian law in Afghanistan,

1. *Demands* that the Taliban, as well as other Afghan factions, stop fighting, conclude a ceasefire and resume negotiations without delay and preconditions under United Nations auspices, and cooperate with the aim of creating a broad-based and fully representative government, which would protect the rights of all Afghans and observe the international obligations of Afghanistan;

2. *Welcomes* the progress made by the Special Envoy of the Secretary-General in his efforts based on resolution 1193 (1998) and its relevant preceding resolutions to reduce tensions in the region and towards improving the human rights and humanitarian situation in Afghanistan and calls upon all concerned to implement fully the commitments they have already entered into;

3. *Reiterates* its very strong support and appreciation for the continuing efforts of the Special Envoy of the Secretary-General to secure the full implementation of its resolutions and demands that all parties, in particular the Taliban, cooperate in good faith with these efforts;

4. *Reiterates* its strong call on the Taliban to inform the

United Nations without further delay about the results of the investigation into the killing of the two Afghan staff members of the World Food Programme and of the Office of the United Nations High Commissioner for Refugees in Jalalabad, and the Military Adviser to UNSMA in Kabul;

5. *Condemns* the capture by the Taliban of the Consulate-General of the Islamic Republic of Iran and the murder of the Iranian diplomats and a journalist in Mazar-e-Sharif, stresses that these acts constitute flagrant violations of international law, and calls upon the Taliban to cooperate with the United Nations in investigating these crimes with a view to prosecuting those responsible;

6. *Encourages* the Secretary-General to continue his efforts to despatch a mission to Afghanistan to investigate numerous reports of grave breaches and serious violations of international humanitarian law in that country, in particular mass killings and mass graves of prisoners of war and civilians and the destruction of religious sites, and urges all parties, especially the Taliban, to cooperate with this mission, and in particular to assure the safety and freedom of movement of its personnel;

7. *Supports* the Secretary-General's proposal, as contained in his letter to the President of the Security Council of 23 November 1998 (S/1998/1139), to establish within UNSMA, without prejudice to its mandate and taking into account security conditions, a civil affairs unit with the primary objective of monitoring the situation, promoting respect for minimum humanitarian standards and deterring massive and systematic violations of human rights and humanitarian law in the future, and to send an assessment mission to Afghanistan, as soon as security conditions permit, in order to determine the exact mandate, composition and location of the civilian monitors;

8. *Encourages* the initiatives of the "six plus two" group to facilitate the peace process in Afghanistan;

9. *Encourages further* the additional support of other Member States for the peace process in Afghanistan;

10. *Reiterates* its call upon all States to take resolute measures to prohibit their military personnel from planning and participating in military operations in Afghanistan and immediately to end the supply of arms and ammunition to all parties to the conflict;

11. *Urges* all Afghan factions, and in particular the Taliban, to demonstrate their full commitment to the safety and security of all international and humanitarian personnel, which is a prerequisite for their activities in Afghanistan, to facilitate their work and to ensure unimpeded access and adequate conditions for the delivery of aid to all in need of it;

12. *Demands* that the Afghan factions put an end to discrimination against girls and women and other violations of human rights, as well as violations of international humanitarian law, and adhere to the international norms and standards in this sphere;

13. *Demands also* that the Taliban stop providing sanctuary and training for international terrorists and their organizations, and that all Afghan factions cooperate with efforts to bring indicted terrorists to justice;

14. *Demands further* that the Taliban, as well as others, halt the cultivation, production and trafficking of illegal drugs;

15. *Deplores* the failure of the leadership of the Taliban, in particular, to take measures to comply with the demands made in its previous resolutions, especially to conclude a ceasefire and to resume negotiations, and in this context expresses its readiness to consider the imposition of measures, in accordance with its responsibility under the Charter of the United Nations, with the aim of achieving the full implementation of its relevant resolutions;

16. *Decides* to remain actively seized of the matter.

24

Resolution 1189 (1998) Adopted by the Security Council at its 3915th meeting on 13 August 1998

The Security Council,

Deeply disturbed by the indiscriminate and outrageous acts of international terrorism that took place on 7 August 1998 in Nairobi, Kenya and Dar-es-Salaam, Tanzania,

Condemning such acts which have a damaging effect on international relations and jeopardize the security of States,

Convinced that the suppression of acts of international terrorism is essential for the maintenance of international peace and security, and reaffirming the determination of the international community to eliminate international terrorism in all its forms and manifestations,

Also reaffirming the obligations of Member States under the Charter of the United Nations,

Stressing that every Member State has the duty to refrain from organizing, instigating, assisting or participating in terrorist acts in another State or acquiescing in organized activities within its territory directed towards the commission of such acts,

Mindful of General Assembly resolution 52/164 of 15 December 1997 on the International Convention for the Suppression of Terrorist Bombings,

Recalling that, in the statement issued on 31 January 1992 (S/23500) on the occasion of the meeting of the Security Council at the level of Heads of State and Government, the Council expressed its deep concern over acts of international terrorism, and emphasized the need for the international community to deal effectively with all such criminal acts,

Also stressing the need to strengthen international cooperation between States in order to adopt practical and effective measures to prevent, combat and eliminate all forms of terrorism affecting the international community as a whole,

Commending the responses of the Governments of Kenya, Tanzania and the United States of America to the terrorist bomb attacks in Kenya and Tanzania,

Determined to eliminate international terrorism,

1. *Strongly condemns* the terrorist bomb attacks in Nairobi, Kenya and Dar-es-Salaam, Tanzania on 7 August 1998 which claimed hundreds of innocent lives, injured thousands of people and caused massive destruction to property;

2. *Expresses* its deep sorrow, sympathy and condolences to the families of the innocent victims of the terrorist bomb attacks during this difficult time;

3. *Calls upon* all States and international institutions to cooperate with and provide support and assistance to the ongoing investigations in Kenya, Tanzania and the United States to apprehend the perpetrators of these cowardly criminal acts and to bring them swiftly to justice;

4. *Expresses* its sincere gratitude to all States, international institutions and voluntary organizations for their encouragement and timely response to the requests for assistance from the Governments of Kenya and Tanzania, and urges them to assist the affected countries, especially in the reconstruction of infrastructure and disaster preparedness;

5. *Calls upon* all States to adopt, in accordance with international law and as a matter of priority, effective and

practical measures for security cooperation, for the prevention of such acts of terrorism, and for the prosecution and punishment of their perpetrators;

6. *Decides* to remain seized of the matter.

25

Measures to Eliminate International Terrorism (52/165, 15 December 1997)

	Meeting : 72
Adopted without a vote	Report : A/52/653

The General Assembly,

Guided by the purposes and principles of the Charter of the United Nations,

Recalling all its relevant resolutions, including resolution 49/60 of 9 December 1994, by which it adopted the Declaration on Measures to Eliminate International Terrorism, and resolutions 50/53 of 11 December 1995 and 51/210 of 17 December 1996,

Recalling also the Declaration on the Occasion of the Fiftieth Anniversary of the United Nations,[1]

Deeply disturbed by the persistence of terrorist acts, which have taken place worldwide,

Stressing the need further to strengthen international cooperation between States and between international organizations and agencies, regional organizations and arrangements and the United Nations in order to prevent, combat and eliminate terrorism in all its forms and manifestations, wherever and by whomsoever committed,

Mindful of the need to enhance the role of the United Nations and the relevant specialized agencies in combating international terrorism, and of the proposals of the Secretary-General to enhance the role of the Organization in this respect,

Recalling that in the Declaration on Measures to Eliminate International Terrorism contained in the annex to resolution 49/60 the General Assembly encouraged States to review urgently the scope of the existing international legal provisions on the prevention, repression and elimination of terrorism in all its forms and manifestations, with the aim of ensuring that there was a comprehensive legal framework covering all aspects of the matter,

Bearing in mind the possibility of considering in the near future the elaboration of a comprehensive convention on international terrorism,

Having examined the report of the Secretary-General,[2]

1. *Strongly condemns* all acts, methods and practices of terrorism as criminal and unjustifiable, wherever and by whomsoever committed;

2. *Reiterates* that criminal acts intended or calculated to provoke a state of terror in the general public, a group of persons or particular persons for political purposes are in any circumstance unjustifiable, whatever the considerations of a political, philosophical, ideological, racial, ethnic, religious or other nature that may be invoked to justify them;

3. *Reiterates its call* upon all States to adopt further measures in accordance with the relevant provisions of international law, including international standards of human rights, to prevent terrorism and to strengthen international cooperation in combating terrorism and, to that end, to consider, in particular, the implementation of the measures set out in paragraphs 3 (a) to (f) of its resolution 51/210;

4. *Also reiterates its call* upon all States, with the aim of enhancing the efficient implementation of relevant legal instruments, to intensify, as and where appropriate, the exchange of information on facts related to terrorism and, in so doing, to avoid the dissemination of inaccurate or unverified information;

5. *Further reiterates its call* upon States to refrain from financing, encouraging, providing training for or otherwise supporting terrorist activities;

6. *Urges* all States that have not yet done so to consider, as a matter of priority, becoming parties to relevant instruments as referred to in paragraph 6 of resolution 51/210, and calls upon all States to enact, as appropriate, domestic legislation necessary to implement the provisions of those Conventions and Protocols, to ensure that the jurisdiction of their courts enables them to bring to trial the perpetrators of terrorist acts and to cooperate with and provide support and assistance to other States and relevant international and regional organizations to that end;

7. *Reaffirms* the Declaration on Measures to Eliminate International Terrorism contained in the annex to resolution 49/60 and the Declaration to Supplement the 1994 Declaration on Measures to Eliminate International Terrorism contained in the annex to resolution 51/210, and calls upon all States to implement them;

8. *Reaffirms* the mandate of the Ad Hoc Committee established by the General Assembly in its resolution 51/210;

9. *Decides* that the Ad Hoc Committee established by General Assembly resolution 51/210 of 17 December 1996 will meet from 16 February to 27 February 1998 to continue its work in accordance with the mandate provided in paragraph 9 of that resolution, and recommends that the work continue during the fifty-third session of the General Assembly from 28 September to 9 October 1998 within the framework of a working group of the Sixth Committee;

10. *Requests* the Secretary-General to invite the International Atomic Energy Agency to assist the Ad Hoc Committee in its deliberations;

11. *Also requests* the Secretary-General to continue to provide the Ad Hoc Committee with the necessary facilities for the performance of its work;

12. *Requests* the Ad Hoc Committee to report to the General Assembly at its fifty-third session on progress made in accomplishing its mandate;

13. *Recommends* that the Ad Hoc Committee be convened in 1999 to continue its work as referred to in paragraph 9 of resolution 51/210;

14. *Decides* to include in the provisional agenda of its fifty-third session the item entitled "Measures to eliminate international terrorism".

NOTES

1. See resolution 50/6.
2. A/52/304 and Corr.1 and Add.1.

26

Human Rights and Terrorism (52/133, 12 December 1997)

Meeting : 70

Vote : 115-0-57

Report : A/52/644/Add.2

The General Assembly,

Guided by the Charter of the United Nations, the Universal Declaration of Human Rights,[1] the Declaration on Principles of International Law concerning Friendly Relations and Cooperation among States in accordance with the Charter of the United Nations[2] and the International Covenants on Human Rights,[3]

Recalling the Declaration on the Occasion of the Fiftieth Anniversary of the United Nations,[4]

Recalling also the Vienna Declaration and Programme of Action, adopted by the World Conference on Human Rights on 25 June 1993,[5]

Recalling further its resolutions 48/122 of 20 December 1993, 49/185 of 23 December 1994 and 50/186 of 22 December 1995,

Recalling further previous resolutions on human rights and terrorism of the Commission on Human Rights and the Subcommission on Prevention of Discrimination and Protection of Minorities,

Taking into account the fact that acts of terrorism in all its forms and manifestations aimed at the destruction of human rights have continued despite national and international efforts,

Bearing in mind that the most essential and basic human right is the right to life,

Bearing in mind also that terrorism creates an environment that destroys the freedom from fear of the people,

Reiterating that all States have an obligation to promote and protect all human rights and fundamental freedoms, and also that every individual should strive to secure their universal and effective recognition and observance,

Seriously concerned at the gross violations of human rights perpetrated by terrorist groups,

Profoundly deploring the increasing number of innocent persons, including women, children and the elderly, killed, massacred and maimed by terrorists in indiscriminate and random acts of violence and terror, which cannot be justified under any circumstances,

Noting with great concern the growing connection between the terrorist groups and other criminal organizations engaged in the illegal traffic in arms and drugs at the national and international levels, as well as the consequent commission of serious crimes such as murder, extortion, kidnapping, assault, taking of hostages and robbery,

Mindful of the need to protect human rights of and guarantees for the individual in accordance with the relevant human rights principles and instruments, particularly the right to life,

Reaffirming that all measures to counter terrorism must be in strict conformity with the relevant provisions of international law including international human rights standards,

1. *Expresses its solidarity* with the victims of terrorism;

2. *Condemns* the violations of the right to live free from fear and of the right to life, liberty and security;

3. *Reiterates its unequivocal condemnation* of the acts,

methods and practices of terrorism, in all its forms and manifestations, as aimed at the destruction of human rights, fundamental freedoms and democracy, threatening the territorial integrity and security of States, destabilizing legitimately constituted Governments, undermining pluralistic civil society and having adverse consequences for the economic and social development of States;

4. *Calls upon* States to take all necessary and effective measures in accordance with relevant provisions of international law, including international human rights standards, to prevent, combat and eliminate terrorism in all its forms and manifestations, wherever and by whomever committed;

5. *Urges* the international community to enhance cooperation at regional and international levels in the fight against terrorism in accordance with relevant international instruments, including those relating to human rights, with the aim of its eradication;

6. *Condemns* incitement of ethnic hatred, violence and terrorism;

7. *Requests* the Secretary-General to continue to seek the views of Member States on the possible establishment of a voluntary fund for the victims of terrorism, as well as ways and means to rehabilitate the victims of terrorism and to reintegrate them into society;

8. *Also requests* the Secretary-General to seek the views of Member States on the implications of terrorism, in all its forms and manifestations, for the full enjoyment of all human rights and fundamental freedoms, and to submit a report on the subject to the General Assembly at its fifty-fourth session;

9. *Decides* to consider this question at its fifty-fourth session under the item entitled "Human rights questions".

RECORDED VOTE ON RESOLUTION 52/133

In favour : Afghanistan, Albania, Algeria, Angola, Antigua and Barbuda, Azerbaijan, Bahamas, Bahrain, Bangladesh, Barbados, Belarus, Belize, Benin, Bhutan, Bolivia, Botswana,

Brazil, Brunei Darussalam, Burkina Faso, Cameroon, Cape Verde, Chad, China, Colombia, Comoros, Costa Rica, Cote D'Ivoire, Croatia, Cuba, Democratic People's Republic of Korea, Democatic Republic of the Congo, Djibouti, Dominica, Dominican Republic, Ecuador, Egypt, El Salvador, Equatorial Guinea, Eritrea, Ethiopia, Gabon, Georgia, Ghana, Grenada, Guatemala, Guinea, Guinea-Bissau, Guyana, Haiti, Honduras, India, Indonesia, Iran, Jamaica, Jordan, Kazakhstan, Kenya, Kuwait, Lao People's Democratic Republic, Lesotho, Liberia, Libya, Madagascar, Malaysia, Maldives, Mali, Mauritania, Mauritius, Mongolia, Morocco, Mozambique, Myanmar, Namibia, Nepal, Nicaragua, Niger, Nigeria, Oman, Pakistan, Panama, Papua New Guinea, Paraguay, Peru, Philippines, Qatar, Republic of Korea, Republic of the Congo, Russian Federation, St Kitts and Nevis, Saint Lucia, Saudi Arabia, Senegal, Singapore, South Africa, Sri Lanka, Sudan, Suriname, Swaziland, Tajikstan, Thailand, The former Yugoslav Republic of Macedonia, Togo, Trinidad and Tobago, Tunisia, Turkey, Turkmenistan, Uganda, United Arab Emirates, United Republic of Tanzania, Uruguay, Venezuela, Viet Nam, Yemen, Zambia, Zimbabwe

Against : None

Abstaining : Andorra, Argentina, Armenia, Australia, Austria, Belgium, Bulgaria, Canada, Chile, Cyprus, Czech Republic, Denmark, Estonia, Federated States of Micronesia, Fiji, Finland, France, Germany, Greece, Hungary, Iceland, Ireland, Israel, Italy, Japan, Kyrgyzstan, Latvia, Lebanon, Liechtenstein, Lithuania, Luxembourg, Malawi, Malta, Marshall Islands, Mexico, Monaco, Netherlands, New Zealand, Norway, Poland, Portugal, Republic of Moldova, Romania, Samoa, San Marino, Sierra Leone, Slovakia, Slovenia, Solomon Islands, Spain, Sweden, Syria, Ukraine, United Kingdom, United States, Uzbekistan, Vanuatu.

Absent : Burundi, Cambodia, Palau, Rwanda, Saint Vincent and the Grenadines, Seychelles.

NOTES

1. Resolution 217 A (III).
2. Resolution 2625 (XXV), annex.
3. Resolution 2200 A (XXI), annex.
4. See resolution 50/6.
5. A/CONF.157/24 (Part I), chap. III.

27

Measures to Eliminate International Terrorism (51/210, 17 December 1996)

The General Assembly,

Recalling its resolution 49/60 of 9 December 1994, by which it adopted the Declaration on Measures to Eliminate International Terrorism, and its resolution 50/53 of 11 December 1995,

Recalling also the Declaration on the Occasion of the Fiftieth Anniversary of the United Nations,

Guided by the purposes and principles of the Charter of the United Nations,

Deeply disturbed by the persistence of terrorist acts, which have taken place worldwide,

Stressing the need further to strengthen international cooperation between States and between international organizations and agencies, regional organizations and arrangements and the United Nations in order to prevent, combat and eliminate terrorism in all its forms and manifestations, wherever and by whomsoever committed,

Mindful of the need to enhance the role of the United Nations and the relevant specialized agencies in combating international terrorism,

Noting, in this context, all regional and international efforts to combat international terrorism, including those of the Organization of African Unity, the Organization of American States, the Organization of the Islamic Conference, the South Asian Association for Regional Cooperation, the European Union, the Council of Europe, the Movement of Non-Aligned Countries and the countries of the group of seven major industrialized countries and the Russian Federation,

Taking note of the report of the Director-General of the United Nations Educational, Scientific and Cultural Organization on educational activities under the project entitled "Towards a culture of peace",

Recalling that in the Declaration on Measures to Eliminate International Terrorism the General Assembly encouraged States to review urgently the scope of the existing international legal provisions on the prevention, repression and elimination of terrorism in all its forms and manifestations, with the aim of ensuring that there was a comprehensive legal framework covering all aspects of the matter,

Bearing in mind the possibility of considering in the future the elaboration of a comprehensive convention on international terrorism,

Noting that terrorist attacks by means of bombs, explosives or other incendiary or lethal devices have become increasingly widespread, and stressing the need to supplement the existing legal instruments in order to address specifically the problem of terrorist attacks carried out by such means,

Recognizing the need to enhance international cooperation to prevent the use of nuclear materials for terrorist purposes and to develop an appropriate legal instrument,

Recognizing also the need to strengthen international cooperation to prevent the use of chemical and biological materials for terrorist purposes,

Convinced of the need to implement effectively and

supplement the provisions of the Declaration on Measures to Eliminate International Terrorism,

Having examined the report of the Secretary-General,

I

1. Strongly condemns all acts, methods and practices of terrorism as criminal and unjustifiable, wherever and by whomsoever committed;

2. Reiterates that criminal acts intended or calculated to provoke a state of terror in the general public, a group of persons or particular persons for political purposes are in any circumstance unjustifiable, whatever the considerations of a political, philosophical, ideological, racial, ethnic, religious or other nature that may be invoked to justify them;

3. Calls upon all States to adopt further measures in accordance with the relevant provisions of international law, including international standards of human rights, to prevent terrorism and to strengthen international cooperation in combating terrorism and, to that end, to consider the adoption of measures such as those contained in the official document adopted by the group of seven major industrialized countries and the Russian Federation at the Ministerial Conference on Terrorism, held in Paris on 30 July 1996, and the plan of action adopted by the Inter-American Specialized Conference on Terrorism, held at Lima from 23 to 26 April 1996 under the auspices of the Organization of American States, and in particular calls upon all States :

(a) To recommend that relevant security officials undertake consultations to improve the capability of Governments to prevent, investigate and respond to terrorist attacks on public facilities, in particular means of public transport, and to cooperate with other Governments in this respect;

(b) To accelerate research and development regarding methods of detection of explosives and other harmful substances that can cause death or injury, undertake consultations on the development of standards for marking explosives in order to identify their origin in post-blast investigations, and promote cooperation and transfer of technology, equipment and related materials, where appropriate;

(c) To note the risk of terrorists using electronic or wire communications systems and networks to carry out criminal acts and the need to find means, consistent with national law, to prevent such criminality and to promote cooperation where appropriate;

(d) To investigate, when sufficient justification exists according to national laws, and acting within their jurisdiction and through appropriate channels of international cooperation, the abuse of organizations, groups or associations, including those with charitable, social or cultural goals, by terrorists who use them as a cover for their own activities;

(e) To develop, if necessary, especially by entering into bilateral and multilateral agreements and arrangements, mutual legal assistance procedures aimed at facilitating and speeding investigations and collecting evidence, as well as cooperation between law enforcement agencies in order to detect and prevent terrorist acts;

(f) To take steps to prevent and counteract, through appropriate domestic measures, the financing of terrorists and terrorist organizations, whether such financing is direct or indirect through organizations which also have or claim to have charitable, social or cultural goals or which are also engaged in unlawful activities such as illicit arms trafficking, drug dealing and racketeering, including the exploitation of persons for purposes of funding terrorist activities, and in particular to consider, where appropriate, adopting regulatory measures to prevent and counteract movements of funds suspected to be intended for terrorist purposes without impeding in any way the freedom of legitimate capital movements and to intensify the exchange of information concerning international movements of such funds;

4. Also calls upon all States, with the aim of enhancing the efficient implementation of relevant legal instruments, to intensify, as and where appropriate, the exchange of information on facts related to terrorism and, in so doing, to avoid the dissemination of inaccurate or unverified information;

5. Reiterates its call upon States to refrain from financing, encouraging, providing training for or otherwise supporting terrorist activities;

6. Urges all States that have not yet done so to consider, as a matter of priority, becoming parties to the Convention on Offences and Certain Other Acts Committed on Board Aircraft, signed at Tokyo on 14 September 1963, the Convention for the Suppression of Unlawful Seizure of Aircraft, signed at The Hague on 16 December 1970, the Convention for the Suppression of Unlawful Acts against the Safety of Civil Aviation, concluded at Montreal on 23 September 1971, the Convention on the Prevention and Punishment of Crimes against Internationally Protected Persons, including Diplomatic Agents, adopted in New York on 14 December 1973, the International Convention against the Taking of Hostages, adopted in New York on 17 December 1979, the Convention on the Physical Protection of Nuclear Material, signed at Vienna on 3 March 1980, the Protocol for the Suppression of Unlawful Acts of Violence at Airports Serving International Civil Aviation, supplementary to the Convention for the Suppression of Unlawful Acts against the Safety of Civil Aviation, signed at Montreal on 24 February 1988, the Convention for the Suppression of Unlawful Acts against the Safety of Maritime Navigation, done at Rome on 10 March 1988, the Protocol for the Suppression of Unlawful Acts against the Safety of Fixed Platforms located on the Continental Shelf, done at Rome on 10 March 1988, and the Convention on the Marking of Plastic Explosives for the

Purpose of Detection, done at Montreal on 1 March 1991, and calls upon all States to enact, as appropriate, domestic legislation necessary to implement the provisions of those Conventions and Protocols, to ensure that the jurisdiction of their courts enables them to bring to trial the perpetrators of terrorist acts and to provide support and assistance to other Governments for those purposes;

II

7. Reaffirms the Declaration on Measures to Eliminate International Terrorism contained in the annex to resolution 49/60;

8. Approves the Declaration to Supplement the 1994 Declaration on Measures to Eliminate International Terrorism, the text of which is annexed to the present resolution;

III

9. Decides to establish an Ad Hoc Committee, open to all States Members of the United Nations or members of specialized agencies or of the International Atomic Energy Agency, to elaborate an international convention for the suppression of terrorist bombings and, subsequently, an international convention for the suppression of acts of nuclear terrorism, to supplement related existing international instruments, and thereafter to address means of further developing a comprehensive legal framework of conventions dealing with international terrorism;

10. Decides also that the Ad Hoc Committee will meet from 24 February to 7 March 1997 to prepare the text of a draft international convention for the suppression of terrorist bombings, and recommends that work continue during the fifty-second session of the General Assembly from 22 September to 3 October 1997 in the framework of a working group of the Sixth Committee;

11. Requests the Secretary-General to provide the Ad Hoc Committee with the necessary facilities for the performance of its work;

12. Requests the Ad Hoc Committee to report to the General Assembly at its fifty-second session on progress made towards the elaboration of the draft convention;

13. Recommends that the Ad Hoc Committee be convened in 1998 to continue its work as referred to in paragraph 9 above;

IV

14. Decides to include in the provisional agenda of its fifty-second session the item entitled "Measures to eliminate international terrorism".

ANNEX

Declaration to Supplement the 1994 Declaration on Measures to Eliminate International Terrorism

The General Assembly,

Guided by the purposes and principles of the Charter of the United Nations,

Recalling the Declaration on Measures to Eliminate International Terrorism adopted by the General Assembly by its resolution 49/60 of 9 December 1994,

Recalling also the Declaration on the Occasion of the Fiftieth Anniversary of the United Nations,

Deeply disturbed by the worldwide persistence of acts of international terrorism in all its forms and manifestations, including those in which States are directly or indirectly involved, which endanger or take innocent lives, have a deleterious effect on international relations and may jeopardize the security of States,

Underlining the importance of States developing extradition agreements or arrangements as necessary in order to ensure that those responsible for terrorist acts are brought to justice,

Noting that the Convention relating to the Status of Refugees, done at Geneva on 28 July 1951, does not provide a basis for the protection of perpetrators of terrorist acts, noting also in this context articles 1, 2, 32 and 33 of the Convention, and emphasizing in this regard the need for States parties to ensure the proper application of the Convention,

Stressing the importance of full compliance by States with their obligations under the provisions of the 1951 Convention and the 1967 Protocol relating to the Status of Refugees, including the principle of non-refoulement of refugees to places where their life or freedom would be threatened on account of their race, religion, nationality, membership in a particular social group or political opinion, and affirming that the present Declaration does not affect the protection afforded under the terms of the Convention and Protocol and other provisions of international law,

Recalling article 4 of the Declaration on Territorial Asylum adopted by the General Assembly by its resolution 2312 (XXII) of 14 December 1967,

Stressing the need further to strengthen international cooperation between States in order to prevent, combat and eliminate terrorism in all its forms and manifestations,

Solemnly declares the following :

1. The States Members of the United Nations solemnly reaffirm their unequivocal condemnation of all acts, methods and practices of terrorism as criminal and unjustifiable, wherever and by whomsoever committed, including those which jeopardize friendly relations among States and peoples and threaten the territorial integrity and security of States;

2. The States Members of the United Nations reaffirm that acts, methods and practices of terrorism are contrary to the purposes and principles of the United Nations; they declare that knowingly financing, planning and inciting terrorist acts are also contrary to the purposes and principles of the United Nations;

3. The States Members of the United Nations reaffirm that States should take appropriate measures in conformity with the relevant provisions of national and international law, including

international standards of human rights, before granting refugee status, for the purpose of ensuring that the asylum-seeker has not participated in terrorist acts, considering in this regard relevant information as to whether the asylum-seeker is subject to investigation for or is charged with or has been convicted of offences connected with terrorism and, after granting refugee status, for the purpose of ensuring that that status is not used for the purpose of preparing or organizing terrorist acts intended to be committed against other States or their citizens;

4. The States Members of the United Nations emphasize that asylum-seekers who are awaiting the processing of their asylum applications may not thereby avoid prosecution for terrorist acts;

5. The States Members of the United Nations reaffirm the importance of ensuring effective cooperation between Member States so that those who have participated in terrorist acts, including their financing, planning or incitement, are brought to justice; they stress their commitment, in conformity with the relevant provisions of international law, including international standards of human rights, to work together to prevent, combat and eliminate terrorism and to take all appropriate steps under their domestic laws either to extradite terrorists or to submit the cases to their competent authorities for the purpose of prosecution;

6. In this context, and while recognizing the sovereign rights of States in extradition matters, States are encouraged, when concluding or applying extradition agreements, not to regard as political offences excluded from the scope of those agreements offences connected with terrorism which endanger or represent a physical threat to the safety and security of persons, whatever the motives which may be invoked to justify them;

7. States are also encouraged, even in the absence of a treaty, to consider facilitating the extradition of persons suspected of having committed terrorist acts, insofar as their national laws permit;

8. The States Members of the United Nations emphasize the importance of taking steps to share expertise and information about terrorists, their movements, their support and their weapons and to share information regarding the investigation and prosecution of terrorist acts.

28

Resolution 1054 (1996) Adopted by the Security Council at its 3660th meeting on 26 April 1996

The Security Council,

Reaffirming its resolution 1044 (1996) of 31 January 1996,

Taking note of the report of the Secretary- General of 11 March 1996 (S/1996/179) submitted pursuant to paragraph 7 of resolution 1044 (1996) and the conclusions contained therein,

Gravely alarmed at the terrorist assassination attempt on the life of the President of the Arab Republic of Egypt, in Addis Ababa, Ethiopia, on 26 June 1995, and *convinced* that those responsible for that act must be brought to justice,

Taking note that the statements of the Organization of African Unity (OAU) Mechanism for Conflict Prevention, Management and Resolution of 11 September 1995, and of 19 December 1995 (S/1996/10, annexes I and II) considered the attempt on the life of President Mubarak as aimed, not only at the President of the Arab Republic of Egypt, and not only at the sovereignty, integrity and stability of Ethiopia, but also at Africa as a whole,

Regretting the fact that the Government of Sudan has not yet complied with the requests of the Central Organ of the OAU set out in those statements,

Taking note of the continued effort of the OAU Secretary-

General to ensure Sudan's compliance with the requests of the Central Organ of the OAU,

Taking note also, with regret, that the Government of Sudan has not responded adequately to the efforts of the OAU,

Deeply alarmed that the Government of Sudan has failed to comply with the requests set out in paragraph 4 of resolution 1044 (1996),

Reaffirming that the suppression of acts of international terrorism, including those in which States are involved is essential for the maintenance of international peace and security,

Determining that the non-compliance by the Government of Sudan with the requests set out in paragraph 4 of resolution 1044 (1996) constitutes a threat to international peace and security,

Determined to eliminate international terrorism and to ensure effective implementation of resolution 1044 (1996) and to that end *acting* under Chapter VII of the Charter of the United Nations,

1. *Demands* that the Government of Sudan comply without further delay with the requests set out in paragraph 4 of resolution 1044 (1996) by :

(a) Taking immediate action to ensure extradition to Ethiopia for prosecution of the three suspects sheltered in Sudan and wanted in connection with the assassination attempt of 26 June 1995 on the life of the President of the Arab Republic of Egypt in Addis Ababa, Ethiopia; and

(b) Desisting from engaging in activities of assisting, supporting and facilitating terrorist activities and from giving shelter and sanctuary to terrorist elements; and henceforth acting in its relations with its neighbours and with others in full conformity with the Charter of the United Nations and with the Charter of the OAU;

2. *Decides* that the provisions set out in paragraph 3 below shall come into force at 00.01 Eastern Standard Time on 10

May 1996, and shall remain in force until the Council determines that the Government of Sudan has complied with paragraph 1 above;

3. *Decides* that all States shall :

(a) Significantly reduce the number and the level of the staff at Sudanese diplomatic missions and consular posts and restrict or control the movement within their territory of all such staff who remain;

(b) Take steps to restrict the entry into or transit through their territory of members of the Government of Sudan, officials of that Government and members of the Sudanese armed forces;

4. *Calls upon* all international and regional organizations not to convene any conference in Sudan;

5. *Calls upon* all States, including States not members of the United Nations and the United Nations specialized agencies to act strictly in conformity with this resolution, notwithstanding the existence of any rights granted or obligations conferred or imposed by any international agreement or of any contract entered into or any licence or permit granted prior to the entry into force of the provisions set out in paragraph 3 above;

6. *Requests* States to report to the Secretary-General of the United Nations within 60 days from the adoption of this resolution on the steps they have taken to give effect to the provisions set out in paragraph 3 above;

7. *Requests* the Secretary-General to submit an initial report to the Council within 60 days of the date specified in paragraph 2 above on the implementation of this resolution;

8. *Decides* to re-examine the matter, 60 days after the date specified in paragraph 2 above and to consider, on the basis of the facts established by the Secretary-General, whether Sudan has complied with the demands in paragraph 1 above and, if not, whether to adopt further measures to ensure its compliance;

9. *Decides* to remain seized of the matter.

29

Statement by the President of the Security Council (4 March 1996)

After consultations of the Security Council held on 4 March 1996, the President of the Security Council issued the following statement to the media on behalf of the Council :

"The members of the Security Council condemn the terrorist attacks in Jerusalem on 3 March and in Tel Aviv on 4 March. They extend their sympathy and deepest condolences to the Government and people of Israel and to the families of the victims. They wish a speedy recovery of the wounded.

"These vile acts had the clear purpose of trying to undermine Middle East peace efforts through such terror. The members of the Security Council reiterate their support for the peace process and call on the parties to consolidate it and to increase their cooperation in curbing violence and combating such terrorism."

30

Resolution 1044 (1996) Adopted by the Security Council at its 3627th meeting on 31 January 1996

The Security Council,

Deeply disturbed by the world-wide persistence of acts of international terrorism in all its forms which endanger or take innocent lives, have a deleterious effect on international relations and jeopardize the security of States,

Recalling the statement made by the President of the Security Council on 31 January 1992 (S/23500) when the Council met at the level of Heads of State and Government in which the members of the Council expressed their deep concern over acts of international terrorism and emphasized the need for the international community to deal effectively with all such acts,

Recalling also the Convention on the Prevention and Punishment of Crimes against Internationally Protected Persons, including Diplomatic Agents, opened for signature at New York on 14 December 1973,

Stressing the imperative need to strengthen international cooperation between States in order to make and adopt practical and effective measures to prevent, combat and eliminate all forms of terrorism that affect the international community as a whole,

Convinced that the suppression of acts of international terrorism, including those in which States are involved, is an essential element for the maintenance of international peace and security,

Gravely alarmed at the terrorist assassination attempt on the life of the President of the Arab Republic of Egypt, in Addis Ababa, Ethiopia, on 26 June 1995, and *convinced* that those responsible for that act must be brought to justice,

Taking note that the Third Extraordinary Session of the Organization of African Unity (OAU) Mechanism for Conflict Prevention, Management and Resolution of 11 September 1995, considered that attack as aimed, not only at the President of the Arab Republic of Egypt, and not only at the sovereignty, integrity and stability of Ethiopia, but also at Africa as a whole,

Taking note also of the statements of the Central Organ of the OAU Mechanism of 11 September 1995 and of 19 December 1995 and *supporting* the implementation of the requests contained therein,

Regretting the fact that the Government of the Sudan has not yet complied with the requests of the Central Organ of the OAU set out in those statements,

Noting the letter from the Permanent Representative of Ethiopia of 9 January 1996 (S/1996/10) to the President of the Security Council,

Noting also the letters from the Permanent Representative of the Sudan of 11 January 1996 (S/1996/22) and 12 January 1996 (S/1996/25) to the President of the Council,

1. *Condemns* the terrorist assassination attempt on the life of the President of the Arab Republic of Egypt in Addis Ababa, Ethiopia, on 26 June 1995;

2. *Strongly deplores* the flagrant violation of the sovereignty and integrity of Ethiopia and the attempt to disturb the peace and security of Ethiopia and the region as a whole;

3. *Commends* the efforts of the Government of Ethiopia to resolve this issue through bilateral and regional arrangements;

4. *Calls upon* the Government of the Sudan to comply with the requests of the Organization of African Unity without further delay to :

(a) Undertake immediate action to extradite to Ethiopia for prosecution the three suspects sheltering in the Sudan and wanted in connection with the assassination attempt on the basis of the 1964 Extradition Treaty between Ethiopia and the Sudan;

(b) Desist from engaging in activities of assisting, supporting and facilitating terrorist activities and from giving shelter and sanctuaries to terrorist elements and act in its relations with its neighbours and with others in full conformity with the Charter of the United Nations and with the Charter of the Organization of African Unity;

5. *Urges* the international community to encourage the Government of the Sudan to respond fully and effectively to the OAU requests;

6. *Welcomes* the efforts of the Secretary-General of the OAU aimed at the implementation of the relevant provisions of the statements of the Central Organ of the OAU Mechanism of 11 September 1995 and of 19 December 1995, and *supports* the OAU in its continued efforts to implement its decisions;

7. *Requests* the Secretary-General in consultation with the OAU to seek the cooperation of the Government of the Sudan in the implementation of this resolution and to report to the Council within 60 days;

8. *Decides* to remain seized of the matter.

31

Human Rights and Terrorism (50/186, 22 December 1995)

The General Assembly,

Guided by the Charter of the United Nations, the Universal Declaration of Human Rights, the Declaration on Principles of International Law concerning Friendly Relations and Cooperation among States in accordance with the Charter of the United Nations and the International Covenants on Human Rights,

Bearing in mind the Declaration on the Occasion of the Fiftieth Anniversary of the United Nations,

Taking into account the fact that acts of terrorism in all its forms and manifestations aimed at the destruction of human rights have continued despite national and international efforts,

Bearing in mind that the most essential and basic human right is the right to life,

Bearing in mind also that terrorism creates an environment that destroys the freedom from fear of the people,

Recalling the Vienna Declaration and Programme of Action, adopted by the World Conference on Human Rights on 25 June 1993,

Recalling also its resolutions 48/122 of 20 December 1993 and 49/185 of 23 December 1994,

Taking note of Commission on Human Rights resolution 1995/43 of 3 March 1995,

Reiterating that all States have an obligation to promote and protect human rights and fundamental freedoms, and also that every individual should strive to secure their universal and effective recognition and observance,

Seriously concerned at the gross violations of human rights perpetrated by terrorist groups,

Profoundly deploring the increasing number of innocent persons, including women, children and the elderly, killed, massacred and maimed by terrorists in indiscriminate and random acts of violence and terror, which cannot be justified under any circumstances,

Noting with great concern the growing connection between the terrorist groups and other criminal organizations engaged in the illegal traffic in arms and drugs at the national and international levels, as well as the consequent commission of serious crimes such as murder, extortion, kidnapping, assault, taking of hostages and robbery,

Mindful of the need to protect human rights of and guarantees for the individual in accordance with the relevant international human rights principles and instruments, particularly the right to life,

Reaffirming that all measures to counter terrorism must be in strict conformity with international human rights standards,

1. Expresses its solidarity with the victims of terrorism;

2. Reiterates its unequivocal condemnation of the acts, methods and practices of terrorism as activities aimed at the destruction of human rights, fundamental freedoms and democracy, threatening the territorial integrity and security of States, destabilizing legitimately constituted Governments, undermining pluralistic civil society and having adverse consequences on the economic and social development of States;

3. Calls upon States to take all necessary and effective measures in accordance with international standards of human

rights to prevent, combat and eliminate all acts of terrorism wherever and by whomever committed;

4. Urges the international community to enhance cooperation at regional and international levels in the fight against terrorism in accordance with relevant international instruments, including those relating to human rights, with the aim of its eradication;

5. Condemns incitement of ethnic hatred, violence and terrorism;

6. Requests the Secretary-General to continue to seek the views of Member States on the possible establishment of a United Nations voluntary fund for victims of terrorism, as well as ways and means to rehabilitate the victims of terrorism and to reintegrate them into society, and to submit to the General Assembly at its fifty-second session, for its consideration, a report containing comments made by Member States on the subject;

7. Also requests the Secretary-General to transmit the text of the present resolution to all Member States and to competent specialized agencies and intergovernmental organizations for their consideration;

8. Encourages special rapporteurs, special representatives and working groups of the Commission on Human Rights, as well as treaty bodies, to pay appropriate attention, within their mandates, to the consequences of the acts, methods and practices of terrorist groups;

9. Decides to consider this question at its fifty-second session under the item entitled "Human rights questions".

32

Measures to Eliminate International Terrorism (50/53, 11 December 1995)

The General Assembly,

Recalling its resolution 49/60 of 9 December 1994, by which it adopted the Declaration on Measures to Eliminate International Terrorism,

Recalling also that, in the statement issued on 31 January 1992 by the President of the Security Council on the occasion of the meeting of the Security Council at the level of heads of State and Government, the members of the Council expressed their deep concern over acts of international terrorism, and emphasized the need for the international community to deal effectively with all such acts,

Recalling further the Declaration on the Occasion of the Fiftieth Anniversary of the United Nations,

Deeply disturbed by the persistence of terrorist acts, which have taken place worldwide,

Stressing the need further to strengthen international cooperation between States and between international organizations and agencies, regional organizations and arrangements and the United Nations in order to prevent, combat and eliminate terrorism in all its forms and manifestations,

Having examined the report of the Secretary-General of 24 August 1995,

1. Strongly condemns all acts, methods and practices of terrorism as criminal and unjustifiable;

2. Reiterates that criminal acts intended or calculated to provoke a state of terror in the general public, a group of persons or particular persons for political purposes are in any circumstance unjustifiable, whatever the considerations of a political, philosophical, ideological, racial, ethnic, religious or any other nature that may be invoked to justify them;

3. Reaffirms the Declaration on Measures to Eliminate International Terrorism annexed to resolution 49/60;

4. Urges all States to promote and implement effectively and in good faith the provisions of the Declaration in all its aspects;

5. Also urges all States to strengthen cooperation with one another to ensure that those who participate in terrorist activities, whatever the nature of their participation, find no safe haven anywhere;

6. Calls upon all States to take the necessary steps to implement their obligations under existing international conventions, to observe fully the principles of international law and to contribute to the further development of international law on this matter;

7. Recalls the role of the Security Council in combating international terrorism whenever it poses a threat to international peace and security;

8. Requests the Secretary-General to follow up closely the implementation of the Declaration and to submit an annual report on the implementation of paragraph 10 of the Declaration, taking into account the modalities set out in his report and the views expressed by States in the debate of the Sixth Committee during the fiftieth session of the General Assembly;

9. Decides to include in the provisional agenda of its fifty-first session the item entitled "Measures to eliminate international terrorism".

33

Statement by the President of the Security Council (30 May 1995)

After consultations of the Security Council held on 24 January 1995, the President of the Council made the following statement to the media on behalf of the members of the Council :

> "The members of the Security Council strongly condemn the terrorist attack which took place in Nordiya, Israel last Sunday, 22 January 1995, with the clear purpose of trying to undermine the Middle East peace efforts.
>
> "The members of the Security Council extend their condolences to the families of those who died as a consequence of the explosions and wish a speedy recovery of the wounded.
>
> "The members of the Security Council call upon all parties to continue their efforts to consolidate the peace process. The members of the Security Council believe that common ground can only be found through the practice of dialogue, respect and tolerance."

34

Human Rights and Terrorism (49/185, 23 December 1994)

The General Assembly,

Guided by the principles embodied in the Charter of the United Nations, the Universal Declaration of Human Rights and the International Covenants on Human Rights,

Bearing in mind that the most essential and basic human right is the right to life,

Recalling the Vienna Declaration and Programme of Action, adopted by the World Conference on Human Rights on 25 June 1993,

Recalling also its resolution 48/122 of 20 December 1993,

Taking note of Commission on Human Rights resolution 1994/46 of 4 March 1994 and resolution 1994/18 of 25 August 1994 of the Subcommission on Prevention of Discrimination and Protection of Minorities,

Reiterating that all Member States have an obligation to promote and protect human rights and fundamental freedoms, and also that every individual should strive to secure their universal and effective recognition and observance,

Seriously concerned at the gross violations of human rights perpetrated by terrorist groups,

Profoundly deploring the increasing number of innocent persons, including women, children and the elderly, killed, massacred and maimed by terrorists in indiscriminate and random acts of violence and terror, which cannot be justified under any circumstances,

Noting with great concern the growing connection between the terrorist groups and the illegal traffic in arms and drugs, as well as the consequent commission of serious crimes such as murder, kidnapping, assault and robbery,

Mindful of the need to protect human rights of and guarantees for the individual in accordance with the relevant international human rights principles and instruments, particularly the right to life,

1. Reiterates its unequivocal condemnation of all acts, methods and practices of terrorism, as activities aimed at the destruction of human rights, fundamental freedoms and democracy, threatening the territorial integrity and security of States, destabilizing legitimately constituted Governments, undermining pluralistic civil society and having adverse consequences on the economic and social development of States;

2. Expresses its solidarity with the victims of terrorism;

3. Calls upon States to take all necessary and effective measures in accordance with international standards of human rights, to prevent, combat and eliminate all acts of terrorism wherever and by whomever committed, and urges the international community to enhance cooperation in the fight against the threat of terrorism at national, regional and international levels;

4. Requests the Secretary-General to seek the views of Member States on the possible establishment of a United Nations voluntary fund for victims of terrorism and to submit to the General Assembly at its fiftieth session, for its consideration, a report containing comments made by Member States on the subject;

5. Also requests the Secretary-General to transmit the text of the present resolution to all Member States and to competent

specialized agencies and intergovernmental organizations for their consideration;

6. Encourages special rapporteurs, special representatives and working groups of the Commission on Human Rights, as well as treaty bodies, to pay appropriate attention, within their mandates, to the consequences of the acts, methods and practices of terrorist groups;

7. Decides to consider this question at its fiftieth session under the item entitled “Human rights questions”.

35

Measures to Eliminate International Terrorism (49/60, 9 December 1994)

The General Assembly,

Recalling its resolution 46/51 of 9 December 1991 and its decision 48/411 of 9 December 1993,

Taking note of the report of the Secretary-General,

Having considered in depth the question of measures to eliminate international terrorism,

Convinced that the adoption of the declaration on measures to eliminate international terrorism should contribute to the enhancement of the struggle against international terrorism,

1. Approves the Declaration on Measures to Eliminate International Terrorism, the text of which is annexed to the present resolution;

2. Invites the Secretary-General to inform all States, the Security Council, the International Court of Justice and the relevant specialized agencies, organizations and organisms of the adoption of the Declaration;

3. Urges that every effort be made in order that the Declaration becomes generally known and is observed and implemented in full;

4. Urges States, in accordance with the provisions of the

Declaration, to take all appropriate measures at the national and international levels to eliminate terrorism;

5. Invites the Secretary-General to follow up closely the implementation of the present resolution and the Declaration, and to submit to the General Assembly at its fiftieth session a report thereon, relating, in particular, to the modalities of implementation of paragraph 10 of the Declaration;

6. Decides to include in the provisional agenda of its fiftieth session the item entitled "Measures to eliminate international terrorism", in order to examine the report of the Secretary-General requested in paragraph 5 above, without prejudice to the annual or biennial consideration of the item.

ANNEX

Declaration on Measures to Eliminate International Terrorism

The General Assembly,

Guided by the purposes and principles of the Charter of the United Nations,

Recalling the Declaration on Principles of International Law concerning Friendly Relations and Cooperation among States in accordance with the Charter of the United Nations, the Declaration on the Strengthening of International Security, the Definition of Aggression, the Declaration on the Enhancement of the Effectiveness of the Principle of Refraining from the Threat or Use of Force in International Relations, the Vienna Declaration and Programme of Action, adopted by the World Conference on Human Rights, the International Covenant on Economic, Social and Cultural Rights and the International Covenant on Civil and Political Rights,

Deeply disturbed by the world-wide persistence of acts of international terrorism in all its forms and manifestations, including those in which States are directly or indirectly involved, which endanger or take innocent lives, have a deleterious effect on international relations and may jeopardize the security of States,

Deeply concerned by the increase, in many regions of the world, of acts of terrorism based on intolerance or extremism,

Concerned at the growing and dangerous links between terrorist groups and drug traffickers and their paramilitary gangs, which have resorted to all types of violence, thus endangering the constitutional order of States and violating basic human rights,

Convinced of the desirability for closer coordination and cooperation among States in combating crimes closely connected with terrorism, including drug trafficking, unlawful arms trade, money laundering and smuggling of nuclear and other potentially deadly materials, and bearing in mind the role that could be played by both the United Nations and regional organizations in this respect,

Firmly determined to eliminate international terrorism in all its forms and manifestations,

Convinced also that the suppression of acts of international terrorism, including those in which States are directly or indirectly involved, is an essential element for the maintenance of international peace and security,

Convinced further that those responsible for acts of international terrorism must be brought to justice,

Stressing the imperative need to further strengthen international cooperation between States in order to take and adopt practical and effective measures to prevent, combat and eliminate all forms of terrorism that affect the international community as a whole,

Conscious of the important role that might be played by the United Nations, the relevant specialized agencies and States in fostering widespread cooperation in preventing and combating international terrorism, inter alia, by increasing public awareness of the problem,

Recalling the existing international treaties relating to various aspects of the problem of international terrorism, inter alia, the Convention on Offences and Certain Other Acts

Committed on Board Aircraft, signed at Tokyo on 14 September 1963, the Convention for the Suppression of Unlawful Seizure of Aircraft, signed at The Hague on 16 December 1970, the Convention for the Suppression of Unlawful Acts against the Safety of Civil Aviation, concluded at Montreal on 23 September 1971, the Convention on the Prevention and Punishment of Crimes against Internationally Protected Persons, including Diplomatic Agents, adopted in New York on 14 December 1973, the International Convention against the Taking of Hostages, adopted in New York on 17 December 1979, the Convention on the Physical Protection of Nuclear Material, adopted at Vienna on 3 March 1980, the Protocol for the Suppression of Unlawful Acts of Violence at Airports Serving International Civil Aviation, supplementary to the Convention for the Suppression of Unlawful Acts against the Safety of Civil Aviation, signed at Montreal on 24 February 1988, the Convention for the Suppression of Unlawful Acts against the Safety of Maritime Navigation, done at Rome on 10 March 1988, the Protocol for the Suppression of Unlawful Acts against the Safety of Fixed Platforms located on the Continental Shelf, done at Rome on 10 March 1988, and the Convention on the Marking of Plastic Explosives for the Purpose of Detection, done at Montreal on 1 March 1991,

Welcoming the conclusion of regional agreements and mutually agreed declarations to combat and eliminate terrorism in all its forms and manifestations,

Convinced of the desirability of keeping under review the scope of existing international legal provisions to combat terrorism in all its forms and manifestations, with the aim of ensuring a comprehensive legal framework for the prevention and elimination of terrorism,

Solemnly declares the following :

I

1. The States Members of the United Nations solemnly reaffirm their unequivocal condemnation of all acts, methods

and practices of terrorism, as criminal and unjustifiable, wherever and by whomever committed, including those which jeopardize the friendly relations among States and peoples and threaten the territorial integrity and security of States;

2. Acts, methods and practices of terrorism constitute a grave violation of the purposes and principles of the United Nations, which may pose a threat to international peace and security, jeopardize friendly relations among States, hinder international cooperation and aim at the destruction of human rights, fundamental freedoms and the democratic bases of society;

3. Criminal acts intended or calculated to provoke a state of terror in the general public, a group of persons or particular persons for political purposes are in any circumstance unjustifiable, whatever the considerations of a political, philosophical, ideological, racial, ethnic, religious or any other nature that may be invoked to justify them;

II

4. States, guided by the purposes and principles of the Charter of the United Nations and other relevant rules of international law, must refrain from organizing, instigating, assisting or participating in terrorist acts in territories of other States, or from acquiescing in or encouraging activities within their territories directed towards the commission of such acts;

5. States must also fulfil their obligations under the Charter of the United Nations and other provisions of international law with respect to combating international terrorism and are urged to take effective and resolute measures in accordance with the relevant provisions of international law and international standards of human rights for the speedy and final elimination of international terrorism, in particular :

(a) To refrain from organizing, instigating, facilitating, financing, encouraging or tolerating terrorist activities and to take appropriate practical measures to ensure that their respective territories are not used for terrorist installations or training camps, or for the preparation or organization of terrorist acts intended to be committed against other States or their citizens;

(b) To ensure the apprehension and prosecution or extradition of perpetrators of terrorist acts, in accordance with the relevant provisions of their national law;

(c) To endeavour to conclude special agreements to that effect on a bilateral, regional and multilateral basis, and to prepare, to that effect, model agreements on cooperation;

(d) To cooperate with one another in exchanging relevant information concerning the prevention and combating of terrorism;

(e) To take promptly all steps necessary to implement the existing international conventions on this subject to which they are parties, including the harmonization of their domestic legislation with those conventions;

(f) To take appropriate measures, before granting asylum, for the purpose of ensuring that the asylum seeker has not engaged in terrorist activities and, after granting asylum, for the purpose of ensuring that the refugee status is not used in a manner contrary to the provisions set out in subparagraph (a) above;

6. In order to combat effectively the increase in, and the growing international character and effects of, acts of terrorism, States should enhance their cooperation in this area through, in particular, systematizing the exchange of information concerning the prevention and combating of terrorism, as well as by effective implementation of the relevant international conventions and conclusion of mutual judicial assistance and extradition agreements on a bilateral, regional and multilateral basis;

7. In this context, States are encouraged to review urgently the scope of the existing international legal provisions on the prevention, repression and elimination of terrorism in all its forms and manifestations, with the aim of ensuring that there

is a comprehensive legal framework covering all aspects of the matter;

8. Furthermore States that have not yet done so are urged to consider, as a matter of priority, becoming parties to the international conventions and protocols relating to various aspects of international terrorism referred to in the preamble to the present Declaration;

III

9. The United Nations, the relevant specialized agencies and intergovernmental organizations and other relevant bodies must make every effort with a view to promoting measures to combat and eliminate acts of terrorism and to strengthening their role in this field;

10. The Secretary-General should assist in the implementation of the present Declaration by taking, within existing resources, the following practical measures to enhance international cooperation :

(a) A collection of data on the status and implementation of existing multilateral, regional and bilateral agreements relating to international terrorism, including information on incidents caused by international terrorism and criminal prosecutions and sentencing, based on information received from the depositaries of those agreements and from Member States;

(b) A compendium of national laws and regulations regarding the prevention and suppression of international terrorism in all its forms and manifestations, based on information received from Member States;

(c) An analytical review of existing international legal instruments relating to international terrorism, in order to assist States in identifying aspects of this matter that have not been covered by such instruments and could be addressed to develop further a comprehensive legal framework of conventions dealing with international terrorism;

(d) A review of existing possibilities within the United Nations system for assisting States in organizing workshops and training courses on combating crimes connected with international terrorism;

IV

11. All States are urged to promote and implement in good faith and effectively the provisions of the present Declaration in all its aspects;

12. Emphasis is placed on the need to pursue efforts aiming at eliminating definitively all acts of terrorism by the strengthening of international cooperation and progressive development of international law and its codification, as well as by enhancement of coordination between, and increase of the efficiency of, the United Nations and the relevant specialized agencies, organizations and bodies.

36

Statement by the President of the Security Council (29 July 1994)

After consultations of the Council held on 29 July 1994, the President of the Security Council made the following statement to the media on behalf of the Council :

> "The members of the Security Council recall the statement issued on the occasion of the Security Council Summit of 31 January 1992 (S/23500), expressing deep concern over acts of international terrorism, and emphasizing the need for the international community to deal effectively with all such acts.
>
> "The members of the Security Council strongly condemn the terrorist attack which took place in Buenos Aires, Argentina on 18 July 1994, which resulted in great loss of human life.
>
> "The members of the Security Council express their sympathy and condolences to the victims and their families and to the people and Government of Argentina, who have suffered the consequences of this terrorist act.
>
> "The members of the Security Council also strongly condemn the terrorist attacks in London on 26 and 27 July 1994, and express their sympathy to the

victims and their families, and to the people and Government of the United Kingdom.

"The members of the Security Council demand an immediate end to all such terrorist attacks. They stress the need to strengthen international cooperation in order to take full and effective measures to prevent, combat and eliminate all forms of terrorism, which affect the international community as a whole."

37

Human Rights and Terrorism (48/122, 20 December 1993)

The General Assembly,

Guided by the principles embodied in the Charter of the United Nations, the Universal Declaration of Human Rights and the International Covenants on Human Rights,

Bearing in mind that the most essential and basic human right is the right to life,

Bearing in mind the Vienna Declaration and Programme of Action, adopted by the World Conference on Human Rights, held at Vienna from 14 to 25 June 1993,

Reiterating that all Member States have an obligation to promote and protect human rights and fundamental freedoms, and also that every individual should strive to secure their universal and effective recognition and observance,

Seriously concerned at the gross violations of human rights perpetrated by terrorist groups,

Profoundly deploring the increasing number of innocent persons, including women, children and the elderly, killed, massacred and maimed by terrorists in indiscriminate and random acts of violence and terror, which cannot be justified under any circumstances,

Noting with great concern the growing connection between the terrorist groups and the illegal traffic in arms and drugs,

Mindful of the need to protect human rights of and guarantees for the individual in accordance with the relevant international human rights principles and instruments, particularly the right to life,

1. *Unequivocally condemns* all acts, methods and practices of terrorism in all its forms and manifestations, wherever and by whomever committed, as activities aimed at the destruction of human rights, fundamental freedoms and democracy, threatening the territorial integrity and security of States, destabilizing legitimately constituted Governments, undermining pluralistic civil society and having adverse consequences on the economic and social development of States;

2. *Calls upon* States, in accordance with international standards of human rights, to take all necessary and effective measures to prevent, combat and eliminate terrorism;

3. *Urges* the international community to enhance cooperation in the fight against the threat of terrorism at national, regional and international levels;

4. *Requests* the Secretary-General to transmit the text of the present resolution to all Member States and to competent specialized agencies and intergovernmental organizations;

5. *Decides* to consider this question at its forty-ninth session under the item entitled "Human rights questions".

38

Resolution 883 (1993) Adopted by the Security Council at its 3312th meeting, on 11 November 1993

The Security Council,

Reaffirming its resolutions 731 (1992) of 21 January 1992 and 748 (1992) of 31 March 1992,

Deeply concerned that after more than twenty months the Libyan Government has not fully complied with these resolutions,

Determined to eliminate international terrorism,

Convinced that those responsible for acts of international terrorism must be brought to justice,

Convinced also that the suppression of acts of international terrorism, including those in which States are directly or indirectly involved, is essential for the maintenance of international peace and security,

Determining, in this context, that the continued failure by the Libyan Government to demonstrate by concrete actions its renunciation of terrorism, and in particular its continued failure to respond fully and effectively to the requests and decisions in resolutions 731 (1992) and 748 (1992), constitute a threat to international peace and security,

Taking note of the letters to the Secretary-General dated 29 September and 1 October 1993 from the Secretary of the General People's Committee for Foreign Liaison and International

Cooperation of Libya (S/26523) and his speech in the General Debate at the forty-eighth session of the General Assembly (A/48/PV.20) in which Libya stated its intention to encourage those charged with the bombing of Pan Am 103 to appear for trial in Scotland and its willingness to cooperate with the competent French authorities in the case of the bombing of UTA 772,

Expressing its gratitude to the Secretary-General for the efforts he has made pursuant to paragraph 4 of resolution 731 (1992),

Recalling the right of States, under Article 50 of the Charter, to consult the Security Council where they find themselves confronted with special economic problems arising from the carrying out of preventive or enforcement measures,

Acting under Chapter VII of the Charter,

1. Demands once again that the Libyan Government comply without any further delay with resolutions 731 (1992) and 748 (1992);

2. Decides, in order to secure compliance by the Libyan Government with the decisions of the Council, to take the following measures, which shall come into force at 00.01 EST on 1 December 1993 unless the Secretary-General has reported to the Council in the terms set out in paragraph 16 below;

3. Decides that all States in which there are funds or other financial resources (including funds derived or generated from property) owned or controlled, directly or indirectly, by :

(a) the Government or public authorities of Libya, or

(b) any Libyan undertaking,

shall freeze such funds and financial resources and ensure that neither they nor any other funds and financial resources are made available, by their nationals or by any persons within their territory, directly or indirectly, to or for the benefit of the Government or public authorities of Libya or any Libyan undertaking, which for the purposes of this paragraph, means any commercial, industrial or public utility undertaking which is owned or controlled, directly or indirectly, by

(i) the Government or public authorities of Libya,

(ii) any entity, wherever located or organized, owned or controlled by (i), or

(iii) any person identified by States as acting on behalf of (i) or (ii) for the purposes of this resolution;

4. Further decides that the measures imposed by paragraph 3 above do not apply to funds or other financial resources derived from the sale or supply of any petroleum or petroleum products, including natural gas and natural gas products, or agricultural products or commodities, originating in Libya and exported therefrom after the time specified in paragraph 2 above, provided that any such funds are paid into separate bank accounts exclusively for these funds;

5. Decides that all States shall prohibit any provision to Libya by their nationals or from their territory of the items listed in the annex to this resolution, as well as the provision of any types of equipment, supplies and grants of licensing arrangements for the manufacture or maintenance of such items;

6. Further decides that, in order to make fully effective the provisions of resolution 748 (1992), all States shall :

(a) require the immediate and complete closure of all Libyan Arab Airlines offices within their territories;

(b) prohibit any commercial transactions with Libyan Arab Airlines by their nationals or from their territory, including the honouring or endorsement of any tickets or other documents issued by that airline;

(c) prohibit, by their nationals or from their territory, the entering into or renewal of arrangements for :

(i) the making available, for operation within Libya, of any aircraft or aircraft components, or

(ii) the provision of engineering or maintenance

servicing of any aircraft or aircraft components within Libya;

(d) prohibit, by their nationals or from their territory, the supply of any materials destined for the construction, improvement or maintenance of Libyan civilian or military airfields and associated facilities and equipment, or of any engineering or other services or components destined for the maintenance of any Libyan civil or military airfields or associated facilities and equipment, except emergency equipment and equipment and services directly related to civilian air traffic control;

(e) prohibit, by their nationals or from their territory, any provision of advice, assistance, or training to Libyan pilots, flight engineers, or aircraft and ground maintenance personnel associated with the operation of aircraft and airfields within Libya;

(f) prohibit, by their nationals or from their territory, any renewal of any direct insurance for Libyan aircraft;

7. Confirms that the decision taken in resolution 748 (1992) that all States shall significantly reduce the level of the staff at Libyan diplomatic missions and consular posts includes all missions and posts established since that decision or after the coming into force of this resolution;

8. Decides that all States, and the Government of Libya, shall take the necessary measures to ensure that no claim shall lie at the instance of the Government or public authorities of Libya, or of any Libyan national, or of any Libyan undertaking as defined in paragraph 3 of this resolution, or of any person claiming through or for the benefit of any such person or undertaking, in connection with any contract or other transaction or commercial operation where its performance was affected by reason of the measures imposed by or pursuant to this resolution or related resolutions;

9. Instructs the Committee established by resolution 748 (1992) to draw up expeditiously guidelines for the implementation

of paragraphs 3 to 7 of this resolution, and to amend and supplement, as appropriate, the guidelines for the implementation of resolution 748 (1992), especially its paragraph 5 (a);

10. Entrusts the Committee established by resolution 748 (1992) with the task of examining possible requests for assistance under the provisions of Article 50 of the Charter of the United Nations and making recommendations to the President of the Security Council for appropriate action;

11. Affirms that nothing in this resolution affects Libya's duty scrupulously to adhere to all of its obligations concerning servicing and repayment of its foreign debt;

12. Calls upon all States, including States not Members of the United Nations, and all international organizations, to act strictly in accordance with the provisions of the present resolution, notwithstanding the existence of any rights or obligations conferred or imposed by any international agreement or any contract entered into or any licence or permit granted prior to the effective time of this resolution;

13. Requests all States to report to the Secretary-General by 15 January 1994 on the measures they have instituted for meeting the obligations set out in paragraphs 3 to 7 above;

14. Invites the Secretary-General to continue his role as set out in paragraph 4 of resolution 731 (1992);

15. Calls again upon all Member States individually and collectively to encourage the Libyan Government to respond fully and effectively to the requests and decisions in resolutions 731 (1992) and 748 (1992);

16. Expresses its readiness to review the measures set forth above and in resolution 748 (1992) with a view to suspending them immediately if the Secretary-General reports to the Council that the Libyan Government has ensured the appearance of those charged with the bombing of Pan Am 103 for trial before the appropriate United Kingdom or United States court and has satisfied the French judicial authorities with respect to the bombing of UTA 772, and with a view to lifting them immediately

when Libya complies fully with the requests and decisions in resolutions 731 (1992) and 748 (1992); and requests the Secretary-General, within 90 days of such suspension, to report to the Council on Libya's compliance with the remaining provisions of its resolutions 731 (1992) and 748 (1992) and, in the case of non-compliance, expresses its resolve to terminate immediately the suspension of these measures;

17. Decides to remain seized of the matter.

39

The SAARC Convention (Suppression of Terrorism) Act, 26th April 1993

1. Act Objective. An Act to give effect to the South Asian Association for Regional Cooperation Convention on Suppression of Terrorism and for matters connected therewith or incidental thereto.

Whereas a Convention on the Suppression of Terrorism was signed on behalf of the Government of India at Kathmandu on the 4th day of November, 1987;

And whereas India, having ratified the said Convention, should make provisions for giving effect thereto and for matters connected therewith or incidental thereto;

Be it enacted by Parliament in the Forty-fourth Year of the Republic of India as follows :

2. Definitions. In this Act, unless the context otherwise requires :

(a) "Convention" means the South Asian Association for Regional Cooperation Convention on Suppression of Terrorism signed at Kathmandu on the 4th day of November, 1987 as set out in the Schedule;

(b) "Convention country" means a country in which the Convention is for the time being in force.

3. Application of the Convention. Notwithstanding anything to the contrary contained in any other law, the provisions of

Articles I to VIII of the Convention shall have the force of law in India.

4. Hostage-taking. (1) Whoever, by force or threat of force or by any other form of intimation, seizes or detains any person and threatens to kill or injure that person with intent to cause a Convention country to do or abstain from doing any act as the means of avoiding the execution of such threat, commits the offence of hostage-taking.

(2) Whoever commits the offence of hostage-taking shall be punished with imprisonment for a term which may extend to ten years, and shall also be liable to fine.

5. Provisions as to Extradition Act. For the purposes of the Extradition Act, 1962 (34 of 1962), in relation to a Convention country, an offence under sub-section (1) of section 4 or any other offence specified in Article I of the Convention, shall not be considered to be an offence of a political character.

6. Offences committed outside India. (1) When an offence under sub-section (1) of section 4 or any other offence specified in Article I of the Convention is committed outside India, —

(a) by a citizen of India, whether on the high seas or elsewhere;

(b) by a person, not being such citizen, on any ship or aircraft, registered in India; or (c) by a person, not being such citizen, in a Convention country, he may be dealt with in respect of such offence as if it had been committed at any place within India at which he may be found.

(2) Notwithstanding anything contained in sub-section (1), the Central Government may, by general or special order published in the Official Gazette, direct that the offence under sub-section (1) of section 4 or any other offence specified in Article I of the Convention may be inquired into or tried at any place within India.

7. Previous sanction necessary for prosecution. No prosecution for an offence under this Act shall be instituted except with the previous sanction of the Central Government and the sanction granted under this section shall be deemed to be a sanction granted under section 188 of the Code of Criminal Procedure, 1973 (2 of 1974).

8. Protection of action taken in good faith. (1) No suit, prosecution or other legal proceeding shall lie against any person for anything which is in good faith done or intended to be done in pursuance of the provisions of this Act.

(2) No suit or other legal proceeding shall lie against the Central Government for any damage caused or likely to be caused for anything which is in good faith done or intended to be done in pursuance of the provisions of this Act.

THE SCHEDULE

SAARC Regional Convention on Suppression of Terrorism. The member-States of the South Asian Association for Regional Co-operation (SAARC).

Mindful of the principles of cooperation enshrined in the SAARC Charter;

Recalling that at the Dhaka Summit on December 7-8, 1985, the Heads of State or Government of the member States of the SAARC recognised the seriousness of the problem of terrorism as it affects the security and stability of the region;

Also Recalling the Bangalore Summit Declaration of 17 November 1986, in which the Heads of State or Government of SAARC agreed that cooperation among SAARC States was vital if terrorism was to be prevented and eliminated from the region; unequivocally condemned all acts, methods and practices of terrorism as criminal and deplored their impact on life and property, socio-economic development, political stability, regional and international peace and cooperation; and recognised the importance of the principles laid down in UN Resolution 2625 (XXV) which among others required that each state should refrain from organising instigating, assisting or participating in acts of civil strife or terrorist acts in another state or acquiesing in organised activities within its territory directed towards the commission of such acts;

Aware of the danger posed by the spread of terrorism and its harmful effect on peace, cooperation, friendship and good neighbourly relations and which could also jeopardise the sovereignty and territorial integrity of states;

Have Resolved to take effective measures to ensure that perpetrators of terroristic acts do not escape prosecution and punishment by providing for their extradition or prosecution, and to this end,

Have Agreed as follows :

Article 1

Subject to the overall requirements of the law of extradition, conduct constituting any of the following offences, according to the law of the Contracting State, shall be regarded as terroristic and for the purpose of extradition shall not be regarded as a political offence or as an offence connected with a political offence or as an offence inspired by political motives :

(a) An offence within the scope of the Convention for the Suppression of Unlawful Seizure of Aircraft, signed at the Hague on December 16, 1970;

(b) An offence within the scope of the Convention for the Suppression of Unlawful Acts against the Safety of Civil Aviation, signed at Montreal on September 23, 1971;

(c) An offence within the scope of the Convention on the Prevention and Punishment of Crimes against Internationally Protected Persons, including Diplomatic Agents, signed at New York on December 14, 1973;

(d) An offence within the scope of any Convention to which the SAARC member States concerned are parties and which obliges the parties to prosecute or grant extradition.

(e) Murder, manslaughter, assault causing bodily harm, kidnapping, hostage-taking and offences relating to firearms, weapons, explosives and dangerous substances when used as a means to perpetrate indiscriminate violence involving death or serious bodily injury to persons or serious damage to property;

(f) An attempt or conspiracy to commit an offence described in sub-paragraphs (a) to (e), aiding, abetting or counselling the commission of such an offence or participating as an accomplice in the offences so described.

Article II

For the purpose of extradition between SAARC member States, any two or more Contracting States may, by agreement, decide to include any other serious offence involving violence, which shall not be regarded as a political offence or an offence connected with a political offence or an offence inspired by political motives.

Article III

1. The provisions of all extradition treaties and arrangements applicable between Contracting States are hereby amended as between Contracting States to the extent that they are incompatible with the Convention.

2. For the purpose of this Convention and to the extent that any offence referred to in Article I or agreed to in terms of Article II is not listed as an extraditable offence in any extradition treaty existing between Contracting States, it shall be deemed to be included as such therein.

3. Contracting States undertake to include these offences as extraditable offences in any future extradition treaty to be concluded between them.

4. If a Contracting State which makes extradition conditional on the existence of a treaty receives a request for extradition from another Contracting State with which it has no extradition

treaty, the requested State may, at its option, consider this Convention as the basis for extradition in respect of the offences set forth in Article I or agreed to in terms of Article II. Extradition shall be subject to the law of the requested State.

5. Contracting States which do not make extradition conditional on the existence of a treaty, shall recognise the offences set forth in Article I or agreed to in terms of Article II as extraditable offences between themselves, subject to the law of the requested State.

Article IV

A Contracting State in whose territory a person suspected of having committed an offence referred to in Article I or agreed to in terms of Article II is found and which has received a request for extradition from another Contracting State, shall, if it does not extradite that person, submit the case without exception and without delay, to its competent authorities, so that prosecution may be considered. These authorities shall take their decisions in the same manner as in the case of any offence of a serious under the law of that State.

Article V

For the purpose of Article IV, each Contracting State may take such measures as it deems appropriate, consistent with its national laws, subject to reciprocity, to exercise its jurisdiction in the case of an offence under Article I or agreed to in terms of Article II.

Article VI

A Contracting State in whose territory an alleged offender is found, shall upon receiving a request for extradition from another Contracting State, take appropriate measures, subject to its national laws, so as to ensure his presence for purposes of extradition or prosecution. Such measures shall immediately be notified to the requesting State.

Article VII

Contracting States shall not be obliged to extradite, if it appears to the requested State that by reason of the trivial nature of the case or by reason of the request for the surrender or return of a fugitive offender not being made in good faith or in the interests of justice or for any other reason it is unjust or inexpedient to surrender or return the fugitive offender.

Article VIII

1. Contracting States shall, subject to their national laws, afford one another the greatest measure of mutual assistance in connection with proceedings brought in respect of the offences referred to in Article I or agreed to in terms of Article II, including the supply of all evidence at their disposal necessary for the proceedings.

2. Contracting States shall cooperate among themselves, to the extent permitted by their national laws, through consultations between appropriate agencies, exchange of information, intelligence and expertise and such other cooperative measures as may be appropriate, with a view to preventing terroristic activities through precautionary measures.

Article IX

1. The Convention shall be open for signature by the member States of SAARC at the SAARC Secretariat in Kathmandu.

2. It shall be subject to ratification. Instruments of Ratification shall be deposited with the Secretary-General of SAARC.

Article X

The Convention shall enter into force on the fifteenth day following the date of the deposit of the seventh Instrument of Ratification with the Secretary-General of SAARC.

Article XI

The Secretary-General of SAARC shall be depository of this Convention and shall notify member States of signatures to this Convention and all deposits of Instruments of Ratification. The Secretary-General shall transit certified copies of such Instruments to each member State. The Secretary-General shall also inform member States of the date on which this Convention will have entered into force in accordance with Article X.

In witness whereof the undersigned, being duly authorised thereto by their respective Governments, have signed this Convention.

Done at Kathmandu on this Fourth Day of November One Thousand Nine Hundred and Eighty Seven, in eight originals, in the English Language, all texts being equally authentic.

40

The Terrorist and Disruptive Activities (Prevention) Act, 1993

An Act further to amend the Terrorist and Disruptive Activities (Prevention) Act, 1987

Be it enacted by Parliament in the Forty-fourth Year of the Republic of India as follows :

1. Short title. This Act may be called the Terrorist and Disruptive Activities (Prevention) Amendment Act, 1993.

2. Amendment of Section 1. In the Terrorist and Disruptive Activities (Prevention) Act, 1987 (hereinafter referred to as the principal Act), in section 1, in sub-section (4) for the words 'six years', the words 'eight years' shall be substituted.

3. Amendment of Section 2. In section 2 of the principal Act, in sub-section (1) after clause (g) the following clause shall be inserted, namely :

"(gg) "property" means property and assets of every description, whether corporeal or incorporeal, movable or immovable, tangible or intangible and deeds and instruments evidencing title to, or interest in, such property or assets, derived or obtained from the terrorist act and includes proceeds of terrorism."

4. Amendment of Section 3. In Section 3 of the principal Act, after sub-section (4) the following sub-sections shall be inserted, namely :

"5. Any person who is a member of a terrorists gang or a terrorists organisation, which is involved in terrorist acts, shall be punishable with imprisonment for a term which shall not be less than five years but which may extend to imprisonment for life and shall also be liable to fine.

6. Whoever holds any property derived or obtained from commission of any terrorist act or has been acquired through the terrorist funds shall be punishable with imprisonment for a term which shall not be less than five years but which may extend to imprisonment for life and shall also be liable to fine".

5. Insertion of new Section 7A. After Section 7 of the principal Act, the following section shall be inserted, namely:

"7A. *Powers of investigating officers.* If an officer investigating an offence committed under this Act has reason to believe that any property in relation to which an investigation is being conducted is a property derived or obtained from the commission of any terrorist act and includes proceeds of terrorism he shall, that the approval of the Superintendent of Police, make an order seizing such property and where it is not practicable to seize such property, he may make an order of attachment directing that such property shall not be transferred or otherwise dealt with except with the prior permission of the officer making such order, or of the Designated Court and a copy of such order shall be served on the persons concerned :

Provided that the investigating officer shall duly inform the Designated Court within forty-eight hours of the attachment of such property and the said Court shall either confirm or revoke the order of attachment so issued."

6. Amendment of Section 15. In Section 15 of the principal Act, —

(a) in sub-section (1), after the words "trial of such

person", the words "or co-accused abettor or conspirator" shall be inserted;

(b) after sub-section (1) the following proviso shall be inserted, namely :

"Provided that co-accused, abetter or conspirator is charged and tried in the same case together with the accused".

7. Amendment of Section 16. In Section 16 of the principal Act for sub-section (1), the following sub-section shall be substituted, namely :

(1) Notwithstanding anything contained in the Code, the proceedings under this Act may be held in camera if the Designated Court so desires".

8. Amendment of Section 20. In Section 20 of the principal Act, in sub-section (4), —

(a) in clause (b) for the words "one year", at both the places where they occur, the words "one hundred and eighty days" shall be substituted;

(b) after clause (b), the following clause shall be inserted, namely :

"(bb) in sub-section (2), after the proviso, the following proviso shall be inserted, namely :

Provided further that, if it is not possible to complete the investigation within the said period of one hundred and eighty days, the Designated Court shall extend the said period up to one year, on the report of the Public Prosecutor indicating the progress of the investigation and the specific reasons for the detention of the accused beyond the said period of one hundred and eighty days".

9. Insertion of new Section 20A. After Section 20 of the principal Act, the following section shall be inserted, namely :

"20A. *Cognizance of offence.* (1) Notwithstanding, anything contained in the Code, no information about the commission of an offence under this Act shall be recorded by the police without the prior approval of the District Superintendent of Police.

2. No court shall take cognizance of any offence under this Act without the previous sanction of the Inspector-General of Police, or as the case may be, the Commissioner of Police."

10. *Amendment of Section 21*. In Section 21 of the principal Act, in sub-section (1), clauses (c) and (d) shall be omitted.

41

Scheme for Surrender-Cum-Rehabilitation of Militants in the North-East : Government of Assam (June 1, 1992 and March 31, 1997)

The following is the text of the scheme announced by the State Government of Assam in 1998 for the surrender and rehabilitation of the terrorists of various outfits. This incidentally was the second such package announced in the State, the first one being the brainchild of the Hiteswar Saikia government. The latter was called the '100 per cent Special Money Margin Scheme' and was implemented between June 1, 1992 and March 31, 1997.

Objectives of the Scheme

1. The objective of the Scheme is to wean away the misguided youth and hardcore militants that have strayed into the folds of militancy and now find themselves trapped into that net. The Scheme also seeks to ensure that the militants who have surrendered do not find it attractive to join militants again.

Eligibility Criteria

2. The Scheme is applicable to those militants who surrender at least with one weapon as mentioned in para 6. However, in exceptional and deserving cases, militants, who surrender without arms, may also be considered for rehabilitation under the

Scheme. The names of such militants would be scrutinised by the Screening Committee and a final view taken by Unified Headquarters or similar body at the State Government headquarters.

Benefits under the Scheme

3. Persons eligible under the Scheme will be initially lodged in a Rehabilitation Camp where they will be imparted training in a trade/vocation of their liking or befitting their aptitude.

4. They shall be paid a monthly stipend for a period of 12 months. The stipend in respect of a surrenderee shall not exceed Rs. 2000 per month. The scale of stipend for various categories of surrenderees will be decided by the State Government in consultation with the Government of India.

5. Board and lodging at the Rehabilitation Camp will be free.

Note 1. The stay of a surrenderee in a Rehabilitation Camp shall not exceed one year. All attempts shall be made to settle the surrenderees during this period. In case of settlement of any surrenderee before the expiry of one year, the stipend shall be stopped with effect from the date of settlement.

Note 2. Minor crime cases against successfully rehabilitated surrenderees will be withdrawn.

Note 3. The surrenderees who have committed heinous crimes like murder, rape, abduction etc. will be subject to the due process of law and surrender shall not imply amnesty from the crimes.

Note 4. A surrenderee who indulge in crime while under rehabilitation shall forfeit the benefits under the Scheme.

Note 5. The agency for rehabilitation may be a suitable NGO and/or the State Government. In case it is an NGO, it will run the Rehabilitation Camp with support from the Security Forces and the Government where required. (A suitable NGO, which has good credentials and willing to work in this sphere, will have to be identified and provided necessary support from the Government). Necessary infrastructure for board, lodging and training of surrenderees shall be provided to the NGO at Government cost.

Incentives for weapons

6. The following incentives have been built into the Scheme for the surrendered weapons/ammunitions :

(i)	Rocket Launchers/UMG/GPMG/PIMCA/ Sniper Rifle	Rs. 25,000 per weapon
(ii)	AK 47/56/74 Rifle	Rs. 15,000 per weapon
(iii)	.303 Rifles/Pistol/Revolver and other service weapon	Rs. 3,000 per weapon
(iv)	Rocket	Rs. 1,000 per weapon
(v)	Grenade/Hand grenade/Stick grenade	Rs. 500 per grenade
(vi)	Remote Control device	Rs. 3000 each
(vii)	Ammunition of all types	Rs. 3 per round
(viii)	Wireless Sets :	Rs. 1000 each
	a. Short range	Rs. 5000 each set
	b. Long range	
(ix)	IED	Rs. 3000 each
(x)	Explosive material	Rs. 1000 per kg.

However, the incentive given for surrender of the aforesaid arms shall be deposited in the form of a Fixed Deposit in the joint name of surrenderee and the NGO/State Government nominee and shall be given to the surrenderee at the time of his leaving the Rehabilitation Camp.

7. The State Governments of the North-East shall implement the Scheme. However, the Government of India shall provide 100% reimbursement for expenditure incurred on the rehabilitation of surrenderees. In view of the financial position of insurgency affected States and also the fact that the NGO's who may undertake rehabilitation work would immediately need some money in advance, it was felt that there shall be provision for giving a part of the rehabilitation money in advance and the rest as reimbursement. Details would be worked out by the

Ministry of Home Affairs in consultation with the Ministry of Finance.

8. The Government of India shall have the right to inspect any of the Camps set up for rehabilitation or transit and to verify any record in this regard.

Procedure

9. The following agencies will be involved in the process of surrender and rehabilitation :

(i) IG (Special Branch) will act as the Surrender and Rehabilitation Officer (S&R Officer) under the Scheme

(ii) Army

(iii) Central Para Military Force

(iv) A nominated NGO

10. Each of the Security Forces will identify one officer of the rank of DIG or equivalent officer as the nodal officer for coordinating surrender and rehabilitation work of militants with respect to their organisation.

11. A militant shall be free to surrender before any unit of the Army/CPMFs, District Magistrate, District SP, Range DIG, IG (Ops), IG (Special Branch), DIG (Special Brach), SPs (Special Branch), SDM, Sub-Divisional Police Officers and other notified officers. The officers for this purpose shall be notified by the State Governments with due approval of the Government of India. A militant may also surrender before any unit if the Army or the CPMFs outside the State. The officer receiving the surrender shall get the details as informed by the surrenderee filled into a prescribed performa and send the same to the S&R Officer and to the nodal officer of the three forces. The nodal officer of each of the organisations will verify the antecedents of the militants from its own sources and his activities and send its specific recommendations to the S&R Officer stating whether the individual could be taken in as surrenderee or not.

12. The officer receiving the surrender will provide immediate security to the surrendered militant and, after getting necessary details for filling up the performa, send him to the Transit Camp to be maintained by the S&R Officer. The board and lodging expenses for the person lodged in the Transit Camp will be borne by the Government. The maximum period within which the decision about a person should be taken would be 15 days.

13. On receiving reports from the four organisations regarding the activities of surrendered person as militant, a Screening Committee headed by the S&R Officer and comprising nodal offices of the four organisations would formally consider the surrender of militant and if accepted, transfer him to the Rehabilitation Camp.

14. Impact assessment of the policy would be done every year to ensure corrective action if required. If the percentage of surrenderees who are successfully rehabilitated at the rehabilitation centre is below 80%, the NGO should be changed.

15. The expenditure during the current financial year, i.e. 1998-99 will be meted out of the sanctioned Budget.

Date of Effect

16. The Scheme will be applicable to those militants who have surrendered/surrender after 1-4-1998. However, the Scheme will have only prospective effect so far as the payment of monthly stipend to the surrenderees is concerned. Similarly, the facilities to be provided to the NGO will be with prospective effect.

Modification in the Scheme

17. The Ministry of Home Affairs may carry out such modifications in the Scheme as may be considered necessary in public interest. The Ministry of Finance will be consulted if any such modification involves financial implications.

42

Resolution 748 (1992) Adopted by the Security Council at its 3063rd meeting on 31 March 1992

The Security Council,

Reaffirming its resolution 731 (1992) of 21 January 1992,

Noting the reports of the Secretary-General (S/23574) and S/23672),

Deeply concerned that the Libyan Government has still not provided a full and effective response to the requests in its resolution 731 of 21 January 1992,

Convinced that the suppression of acts of international terrorism, including those in which States are directly or indirectly involved, is essential for the maintenance of international peace and security,

Recalling that in the statement issued on 31 January 1992 on the occasion of the meeting of the Security Council at the levels of Heads of State and Government the members of the Council expressed their deep concern over acts of international terrorism and emphasized the need for the international community to deal effectively with all such acts,

Reaffirming that, in accordance with the principle in Article 2, paragraph 4, of the Charter of the United Nations, every State has the duty to refrain from organizing, instigating, assisting or participating in terrorist acts in another State or acquiescing in organized activities within its territory directed towards the commission of such acts, when such acts involve a threat or use of force,

Determining in this context that the failure by the Libyan Government to demonstrate, by concrete actions its renunciation of terrorism and in particular its continued failure to respond fully and effectively to the requests in resolution 731 (1992), constitute a threat to international peace and security,

Determined to eliminate international terrorism,

Recalling the right of States, under Article 50 of the Charter, to consult the Security Council where they find themselves confronted with special economic problems arising from the carrying out of preventive or enforcement measures,

Acting under Chapter VII of the Charter of the United Nations,

1. Decides that the Libyan Government must now comply without any further delay with paragraph 3 of resolution 731 (1992) regarding the requests contained in documents S/23306, S/23308 and S/23309;

2. Decides also that the Libyan Government must commit itself definitively to cease all forms of terrorist action and all assistance to terrorist groups and that it must promptly, by concrete actions, demonstrate its renunciation of terrorism;

3. Decides that on 15 April 1992 all States shall adopt the measures set out below, which shall apply until the Security Council decides that the Libyan Government has complied with paragraphs 1 and 2 above;

4. Decides that all States shall :

(a) Deny permission to any aircraft to take off from, land in or overfly their territory if it is destined to land in or has taken off from the territory of Libya, unless the particular flight has been approved on grounds of significant humanitarian need by the Committee established by paragraph 9 below;

(b) Prohibit, by their nationals or from their territory, the supply of any aircraft or aircraft components to Libya, the provision of engineering and maintenance servicing of Libyan aircraft or aircraft components, the certification of air-worthiness for Libyan aircraft, the payment of new claims against existing insurance contracts, and the provision of new direct insurance for Libyan aircraft;

5. Decides further that all States shall :

(a) Prohibit any provision to Libya by their nationals or from their territory of arms and related material of all types, including the sale or transfer of weapons and ammunition, military vehicles and equipment, paramilitary police equipment and spare parts for the aforementioned, as well as the provision of any types of equipment, supplies and grants of licensing arrangements, for the manufacture or maintenance of the aforementioned;

(b) Prohibit any provision to Libya by their nationals or from their territory of technical advice, assistance or training related to the provision, manufacture, maintenance, or use of the items in (a) above;

(c) Withdraw any of their officials or agents present in Libya to advise the Libyan authorities on military matters;

6. Decides also that all States shall :

(a) Significantly reduce the number and the level of the staff at Libyan diplomatic missions and consular posts and restrict or control the movement within their territory of all such staff who remain; in the case of Libyan missions to international organizations, the host State may, as it deems necessary, consult the organization concerned on the measures required to implement this subparagraph;

(b) Prevent the operation of all Libyan Arab Airlines offices;

(c) Take all appropriate steps to deny entry to or expel Libyan nationals who have been denied entry to or expelled from other States because of their involvement in terrorist activities;

7. Calls upon all States, including States not Members of the United Nations, and all international organizations, to act strictly in accordance with the provisions of the present resolution, notwithstanding the existence of any rights or obligations conferred or imposed by any international agreement or any contract entered into or any licence or permit granted before 15 April 1992;

8. Requests all States to report to the Secretary-General by 15 May 1992 on the measures they have instituted for meeting the obligations set out in paragraphs 3 to 7 above;

9. Decides to establish, in accordance with rule 28 of its provisional rules of procedure, a Committee of the Security Council consisting of all the members of the Council, to undertake the following tasks and to report on its work to the Council with its observations and recommendations :

(a) To examine the reports submitted pursuant to paragraph 8 above;

(b) To seek from all States further information regarding the action taken by them concerning the effective implementation of the measures imposed by paragraphs 3 to 7 above;

(c) To consider any information brought to its attention by States concerning violations of the measures imposed by paragraphs 3 to 7 above, and in that context, to make recommendations to the Council on ways to increase their effectiveness;

(d) To recommend appropriate measures in response to violations of the measures imposed by paragraphs 3 to 7 above and provide information on a regular basis to the Secretary-General for general distribution to Member States;

(e) To consider and to decide upon expeditiously any application by States for the approval of flights on grounds of significant humanitarian need in accordance with paragraph 4 above;

(f) To give special attention to any communications in accordance with Article 50 of the Charter of the United Nations from any neighbouring or other States with special economic problems which might arise from the carrying out of the measures imposed by paragraphs 3 to 7 above;

10. Calls upon all States to cooperate fully with the Committee in the fulfilment of its task, including supplying such information as may be sought by the Committee in pursuance of the present resolution;

11. Requests the Secretary-General to provide all necessary assistance to the Committee and to make the necessary arrangements in the Secretariat for this purpose;

12. Invites the Secretary-General to continue his role as set out in paragraph 4 of resolution 731 (1992);

13. Decides that the Security Council shall, every 120 days or sooner should the situation so require, review the measures imposed by paragraphs 3 to 7 above in the light of the compliance by the Libyan Government with paragraphs 1 and 2 above taking into account, as appropriate, any reports provided by the Secretary-General on his role as set out in paragraph 4 of resolution 731 (1992);

14. Decides to remain seized of the matter.

43

Resolution 731 (1992) Adopted by the Security Council at its 3033rd meeting on 21 January 1992

The Security Council,

Deeply disturbed by the world-wide persistence of acts of international terrorism in all its forms, including those in which States are directly or indirectly involved, which endanger or take innocent lives, have a deleterious effect on international relations and jeopardize the security of States,

Deeply concerned by all activities directed against international civil aviation and affirming the right of all States, in accordance with the Charter of the United Nations and relevant principles of international law, to protect their nationals from acts of international terrorism that constitute threats to international peace and security,

Reaffirming its resolution 286 (1970) in which it called on States to take all possible legal steps to prevent any interference with international civil air travel,

Reaffirming also its resolution 635 (1989) in which it condemned all acts of unlawful interference against the security of civil aviation and called upon all States to cooperate in devising and implementing measures to prevent all acts of terrorism, including those involving explosives,

Recalling the statement made on 30 December 1988 by the

President of the Council on behalf of the members of the Council strongly condemning the destruction of Pan Am flight 103 and calling on all States to assist in the apprehension and prosecution of those responsible for this criminal act,

Deeply concerned over results of investigations which implicate officials of the Libyan Government and which are contained in Security Council documents that include the requests addressed to the Libyan authorities by France, the United Kingdom of Great Britain and Northern Ireland and the United States of America in connection with the legal procedures related to the attacks carried out against Pan Am flight 103 and UTA flight 772;

Determined to eliminate international terrorism,

1. *Condemns* the destruction of Pan Am flight 103 and UTA flight 772 and the resultant loss of hundreds of lives;

2. *Strongly deplores* the fact that the Libyan Government has not yet responded effectively to the above requests to cooperate fully in establishing responsibility for the terrorist acts referred to above against Pan Am flight 103 and UTA flight 772;

3. *Urges* the Libyan Government immediately to provide a full and effective response to those requests so as to contribute to the elimination of international terrorism;

4. *Requests* the Secretary-General to seek the cooperation of the Libyan Government to provide a full and effective response to those requests;

5. *Urges* all States individually and collectively to encourage the Libyan Government to respond fully and effectively to those requests;

6. *Decides* to remain seized of the matter.

44

Measures to Eliminate International Terrorism (46/51, 9 December 1991)

The General Assembly,

Recalling its resolutions 3034 (XXVII) of 18 December 1972, 31/102 of 15 December 1976, 32/147 of 16 December 1977, 34/145 of 17 December 1979, 36/109 of 10 December 1981, 38/130 of 19 December 1983, 40/61 of 9 December 1985, 42/159 of 7 December 1987 and 44/29 of 4 December 1989,

Recalling also the recommendations of the Ad Hoc Committee on International Terrorism contained in its report to the General Assembly at its thirty-fourth session,

Recalling further the Declaration on Principles of International Law concerning Friendly Relations and Cooperation among States in accordance with the Charter of the United Nations, the Declaration on the Strengthening of International Security, the Definition of Aggression and relevant instruments on international humanitarian law applicable in armed conflict,

Recalling moreover the existing international conventions relating to various aspects of the problem of international terrorism, inter alia, the Convention on Offences and Certain Other Acts Committed on Board Aircraft, signed at Tokyo on 14 September 1963, the Convention for the Suppression of

Unlawful Seizure of Aircraft, signed at The Hague on 16 December 1970, the Convention for the Suppression of Unlawful Acts against the Safety of Civil Aviation, concluded at Montreal on 23 September 1971, the Convention on the Prevention and Punishment of Crimes against Internationally Protected Persons, including Diplomatic Agents, adopted in New York on 14 December 1973, the International Convention against the Taking of Hostages, adopted in New York on 17 December 1979, the Convention on the Physical Protection of Nuclear Material, adopted at Vienna on 3 March 1980, the Protocol for the Suppression of Unlawful Acts of Violence at Airports Serving International Civil Aviation, supplementary to the Convention for the Suppression of Unlawful Acts against the Safety of Civil Aviation, signed at Montreal on 24 February 1988, the Convention for the Suppression of Unlawful Acts against the Safety of Maritime Navigation, done at Rome on 10 March 1988, the Protocol for the Suppression of Unlawful Acts against the Safety of Fixed Platforms located on the Continental Shelf, done at Rome on 10 March 1988 and the Convention on the Marking of Plastic Explosives for the Purpose of Detection, done at Montreal on 1 March 1991,

Convinced that a policy of firmness and effective measures should be taken in accordance with international law in order that all acts, methods and practices of international terrorism may be brought to an end,

Bearing in mind Security Council resolution 638 (1989) of 31 July 1989 on the taking of hostages,

Deeply disturbed by the world-wide persistence of acts of international terrorism in all its forms, including those in which States are directly or indirectly involved, which endanger or take innocent lives, have a deleterious effect on international relations and may jeopardize the territorial integrity and security of States,

Calling attention to the growing connection between terrorist groups and drug traffickers,

Convinced of the importance of the observance by States of their obligations under the relevant international conventions to ensure that appropriate law enforcement measures are taken in connection with the offences addressed in those conventions,

Convinced also of the importance of expanding and improving international cooperation among States, on a bilateral, regional and multilateral basis, which will contribute to the elimination of acts of international terrorism and their underlying causes and to the prevention and elimination of this criminal scourge,

Convinced further that international cooperation in combating and preventing terrorism will contribute to the strengthening of confidence among States, reduce tensions and create a better climate among them,

Mindful of the need to enhance the role of the United Nations and the relevant specialized agencies in combating international terrorism,

Mindful also of the necessity of maintaining and protecting the basic rights of, and guarantees for, the individual in accordance with the relevant international human rights instruments and generally accepted international standards,

Reaffirming the principle of self-determination of peoples as enshrined in the Charter of the United Nations,

Reaffirming also the inalienable right to self-determination and independence of all peoples under colonial and racist regimes and other forms of alien domination and foreign occupation, and upholding the legitimacy of their struggle, in particular the struggle of national liberation movements, in accordance with the purposes and principles of the Charter and the Declaration on Principles of International Law concerning Friendly Relations and Cooperation among States in accordance with the Charter of the United Nations,

Noting the efforts and important achievements of the International Civil Aviation Organization and the International Maritime Organization in promoting the security of international air and sea transport against acts of terrorism,

Recognizing that the effectiveness of the struggle against terrorism could be enhanced by the establishment of a generally agreed definition of international terrorism,

Taking note of the report of the Secretary-General,

1. Once again unequivocally condemns, as criminal and unjustifiable, all acts, methods and practices of terrorism wherever and by whomever committed, including those which jeopardize the friendly relations among States and their security;

2. Deeply deplores the loss of human lives which results from such acts of terrorism, as well as the pernicious impact of these acts on relations of cooperation among States;

3. Calls upon all States to fulfil their obligations under international law to refrain from organizing, instigating, assisting or participating in terrorist acts in other States, or acquiescing in or encouraging activities within their territory directed towards the commission of such acts;

4. Urges all States to fulfil their obligations under international law and take effective and resolute measures for the speedy and final elimination of international terrorism and to that end, in particular :

(a) To prevent the preparation and organization in their respective territories, for commission within or outside their territories, of terrorist and subversive acts directed against other States and their citizens;

(b) To ensure the apprehension and prosecution or extradition of perpetrators of terrorist acts;

(c) To endeavour to conclude special agreements to that effect on a bilateral, regional and multilateral basis;

(d) To cooperate with one another in exchanging relevant information concerning the prevention and combating of terrorism;

(e) To take promptly all steps necessary to implement the existing international conventions on this subject to which they are parties, including the harmonization of their domestic legislation with those conventions;

5. Appeals to all States that have not yet done so to consider becoming party to the international conventions relating to various aspects of international terrorism referred to in the preamble to the present resolution;

6. Urges all States, unilaterally and in cooperation with other States, as well as relevant United Nations organs, to contribute to the progressive elimination of the causes underlying international terrorism and to pay special attention to all situations, including colonialism, racism and situations involving mass and flagrant violations of human rights and fundamental freedoms and those involving alien domination and foreign occupation, that may give rise to international terrorism and may endanger international peace and security;

7. Firmly calls for the immediate and safe release of all hostages and abducted persons, wherever and by whomever they are being held;

8. Calls upon all States to use their political influence in accordance with the Charter of the United Nations and the principles of international law to secure the safe release of all hostages and abducted persons and to prevent the commission of acts of hostage-taking and abduction;

9. Expresses concern at the growing and dangerous links between terrorist groups, drug traffickers and their paramilitary gangs, which have resorted to all types of violence, thus endangering the constitutional order of States and violating basic human rights;

10. Welcomes the efforts undertaken by the International Civil Aviation Organization aimed at promoting universal acceptance of, and strict compliance with, international air security conventions, and welcomes also the recent adoption of the Convention on the Marking of Plastic Explosives for the Purpose of Detection;

11. Requests the other relevant specialized agencies and

intergovernmental organizations, in particular the International Maritime Organization, the Universal Postal Union, the World Tourism Organization, the International Atomic Energy Agency and the United Nations Educational, Scientific and Cultural Organization, within their respective spheres of competence, to consider what further measures can usefully be taken to combat and eliminate terrorism;

12. Requests the Secretary-General to continue seeking the views of Member States on international terrorism in all its aspects and on ways and means of combating it, including the convening at an appropriate time, under the auspices of the United Nations, of an international conference to deal with international terrorism in the light of the proposal referred to in the penultimate preambular paragraph of resolution 44/29;

13. Also requests the Secretary-General to seek the views of Member States on the proposals contained in his report or made during the debate on this item in the Sixth Committee, and on the ways and means of enhancing the role of the United Nations and the relevant specialized agencies in combating international terrorism;

14. Further requests the Secretary-General to follow up, as appropriate, the implementation of the present resolution and to submit a report in this respect to the General Assembly at its forty-eighth session;

15. Considers that nothing in the present resolution could in any way prejudice the right to self-determination, freedom and independence, as derived from the Charter of the United Nations, of peoples forcibly deprived of that right referred to in the Declaration of Principles of International Law concerning Friendly Relations and Cooperation among States in accordance with the Charter of the United Nations, particularly peoples under colonial and racist regimes or other forms of alien domination, or the right of these peoples to struggle legitimately to this end and to seek and receive support in accordance with the principles of the Charter, the above-mentioned Declaration

and the relevant General Assembly resolutions, including the present resolution;

16. Decides to include in the provisional agenda of its forty-eighth session an item entitled "Measures to eliminate international terrorism".

45

Schengen Accord — Convention Applying the Schengen Agreement of 14 June 1985, 19 June 1990

***

CHAPTER 4 — EXTRADITION

Article 59

1. The provisions of this Chapter are intended to supplement the European Convention of 13 September 1957 on Extradition as well as, in relations between the Contracting Parties which are members of the Benelux Economic Union, Chapter I of the Benelux Treaty on Extradition and Mutual Assistance in Criminal Matters of 27 June 1962, as amended by the Protocol of 11 May 1974, and to facilitate the implementation of these agreements.

2. Paragraph 1 shall not affect the application of the broader provisions of the bilateral agreements in force between Contracting Parties.

Article 60

In relations between two Contracting Parties, one of which is not a party to the European Convention on Extradition of 13 September 1957, the provisions of the said Convention shall apply, subject to the reservations and declarations made at the time of ratifying this Convention or, for Contracting Parties which are not parties to the Convention, at the time of ratifying, approving or accepting the present Convention.

Article 61

The French Republic undertakes to extradite, at the request of one of the Contracting Parties, persons against whom proceedings are being taken for offences punishable under French law by deprivation of liberty or under a detention order for a maximum period of at least two years and under the law of the requesting Contracting Party by deprivation of liberty or under a detention order for a maximum period of at least a year.

Article 62

1. As regards interruption of prescription, only the provisions of the requesting Contracting Party shall apply.

2. An amnesty granted by the requested Contracting Party shall not prevent extradition unless the offence falls within the jurisdiction of that Contracting Party.

3. The absence of a charge or an official notice authorizing proceedings, necessary only under the legislation of the requested Contracting Party, shall not affect the obligation to extradite.

Article 63

The Contracting Parties undertake, in accordance with the Convention and the Treaty referred to in Article 54, to extradite between themselves persons being prosecuted by the legal authorities of the requesting Contracting Party for one of the offences referred to in Article 50(1), or being sought by them for the purposes of execution of a sentence or detention order imposed in respect of such an offence.

Article 64

A report included in the Schengen Information System in accordance with Article 95 shall have the same force as a request for provisional arrest under Article 16 of the European Convention on Extradition of 13 September 1957 or Article 15 of the Benelux Treaty on Extradition and Mutual Assistance in Criminal Matters of 27 June 1962, as amended by the Protocol of 11 May 1974.

Article 65

1. Without prejudice to the option to use the diplomatic channel, requests for extradition and transit shall be sent by the relevant Ministry of the requesting Contracting Party to the relevant Ministry of the requested Contracting Party.

2. The relevant Ministries shall be :

- as regards the Kingdom of Belgium : the Ministry of Justice;
- as regards the Federal Republic of Germany : the Federal Ministry of Justice and the Justice Ministers or Senators of the Federal States;
- as regards the French Republic : the Ministry of Foreign Affairs;
- as regards the Grand Duchy of Luxembourg : the Ministry of Justice;
- as regards the Kingdom of the Netherlands : the Ministry of Justice.

Article 66

1. If the extradition of a wanted person is not obviously prohibited under the laws of the requested Contracting Party, that Contracting Party may authorize extradition without formal extradition proceedings, provided that the wanted person agrees thereto in a statement made before a member of the judiciary after being examined by the latter and informed of his right to formal extradition proceedings. The wanted person may have access to a lawyer during such examination.

2. In cases of extradition under paragraph 1, a wanted person who explicitly states that he will not invoke the rule of speciality may not revoke that statement.

46

Measures to Prevent International Terrorism (44/29, 4 December 1989)

Measures to prevent international terrorism which endangers or takes innocent human lives or jeopardizes fundamental freedoms and study of the underlying causes of those forms of terrorism and acts of violence which lie in misery, frustration, grievance and despair and which cause some people to sacrifice human lives, including their own, in an attempt to effect radical changes :

(a) Report of the Secretary-General;

(b) Convening, under the auspices of the United Nations, of an international conference to define terrorism and differentiate it from the struggle of peoples for national liberation

The General Assembly,

Recalling its resolutions 3034 (XXVII) of 18 December 1972, 31/102 of 15 December 1976, 32/147 of 16 December 1977, 34/145 of 17 December 1979, 36/109 of 10 December 1981, 38/130 of 19 December 1983, 40/61 of 9 December 1985 and 42/159 of 7 December 1987,

Recalling also the recommendations of the Ad Hoc Committee on International Terrorism contained in its report to the General Assembly at its thirty-fourth session,

Recalling further the Declaration on Principles of International Law concerning Friendly Relations and Co-operation among States in accordance with the Charter of the United Nations, the Declaration on the Strengthening of International Security, the Definition of Aggression and relevant instruments on international humanitarian law applicable in armed conflict,

Recalling moreover the existing international conventions relating to various aspects of the problem of international terrorism, inter alia, the Convention on Offences and Certain Other Acts Committed on Board Aircraft, signed at Tokyo on 14 September 1963, the Convention for the Suppression of Unlawful Seizure of Aircraft, signed at The Hague on 16 December 1970, the Convention for the Suppression of Unlawful Acts against the Safety of Civil Aviation, concluded at Montreal on 23 September 1971, the Convention on the Prevention and Punishment of Crimes against Internationally Protected Persons, including Diplomatic Agents, adopted in New York on 14 December 1973, the International Convention against the Taking of Hostages, adopted in New York on 17 December 1979, the Convention on the Physical Protection of Nuclear Material, adopted at Vienna on 3 March 1980, the Protocol for the Suppression of Unlawful Acts of Violence at Airports Serving International Civil Aviation, supplementary to the Convention for the Suppression of Unlawful Acts against the Safety of Civil Aviation, signed at Montreal on 24 February 1988, the Convention for the Suppression of Unlawful Acts against the Safety of Maritime Navigation, done at Rome on 10 March 1988, and the Protocol for the Suppression of Unlawful Acts against the Safety of Fixed Platforms located on the Continental Shelf, done at Rome on 10 March 1988,

Convinced that a policy of firmness and effective measures should be taken in accordance with international law in order that all acts, methods and practices of international terrorism may be brought to an end,

Noting the ongoing work within the International Civil Aviation Organization regarding research as to the detection of plastic or sheet explosives and the devising of an international regime for the marking of such explosives for the purposes of detection, and taking note of Security Council resolution 635 (1989) of 14 June 1989 relating thereto,

Taking note of Security Council resolution 638 (1989) of 31 July 1989 on the taking of hostages,

Deeply disturbed by the world-wide persistence of acts of international terrorism in all its forms, including those in which States are directly or indirectly involved, which endanger or take innocent lives, have a deleterious effect on international relations and may jeopardize the territorial integrity and security of States,

Calling attention to the growing connection between terrorist groups and drug traffickers,

Convinced of the importance of the observance by States of their obligations under the relevant international conventions to ensure that appropriate law-enforcement measures are taken in connection with the offences addressed in those conventions,

Convinced also of the importance of expanding and improving international co-operation among States, on a bilateral, regional and multilateral basis, which will contribute to the elimination of acts of international terrorism and their underlying causes and to the prevention and elimination of this criminal scourge,

Convinced further that international co-operation in combating and preventing terrorism will contribute to the strengthening of confidence among States, reduce tensions and create a better climate among them,

Mindful of the need to enhance the role of the United Nations and the relevant specialized agencies in combating international terrorism,

Mindful also of the necessity of maintaining and protecting the basic rights of, and guarantees for, the individual in accordance with the relevant international human rights instruments and generally accepted international standards,

Reaffirming the principle of self-determination of peoples as enshrined in the Charter of the United Nations,

Reaffirming also the inalienable right to self-determination and independence of all peoples under colonial and racist regimes and other forms of alien domination and foreign occupation, and upholding the legitimacy of their struggle, in particular the struggle of national liberation movements, in accordance with the purposes and principles of the Charter and the Declaration on Principles of International Law concerning Friendly Relations and Co-operation among States in accordance with the Charter of the United Nations,

Noting the efforts and important achievements of the International Civil Aviation Organization and the International Maritime Organization in promoting the security of international air and sea transport against acts of terrorism,

Recognizing that the effectiveness of the struggle against terrorism could be enhanced by the establishment of a generally agreed definition of international terrorism,

Taking into account the proposal made at its forty-second session to hold an international conference on international terrorism, as referred to in agenda item 139 (b),

Taking note of the report of the Secretary-General,

1. Once again unequivocally condemns, as criminal and unjustifiable, all acts, methods and practices of terrorism wherever and by whomever committed, including those which jeopardize the friendly relations among States and their security;

2. Deeply deplores the loss of human lives which results from such acts of terrorism, as well as the pernicious impact of these acts on relations of co-operation among States;

3. Calls upon all States to fulfil their obligations under international law to refrain from organizing, instigating, assisting or participating in terrorist acts in other States, or acquiescing in or encouraging activities within their territory directed towards the commission of such acts;

4. Urges all States to fulfil their obligations under international law and take effective and resolute measures for the speedy and final elimination of international terrorism and to that end, in particular :

(a) To prevent the preparation and organization in their respective territories, for commission within or outside their territories, of terrorist and subversive acts directed against other States and their citizens;

(b) To ensure the apprehension and prosecution or extradition of perpetrators of terrorist acts;

(c) To endeavour to conclude special agreements to that effect on a bilateral, regional and multilateral basis;

(d) To co-operate with one another in exchanging relevant information concerning the prevention and combating of terrorism;

(e) To take promptly all steps necessary to implement the existing international conventions on this subject to which they are parties, including the harmonization of their domestic legislation with those conventions;

5. Appeals to all States that have not yet done so to consider becoming party to the international conventions relating to various aspects of international terrorism referred to in the preamble to the present resolution;

6. Urges all States, unilaterally and in co-operation with other States, as well as relevant United Nations organs, to contribute to the progressive elimination of the causes underlying international terrorism and to pay special attention to all situations, including colonialism, racism and situations involving mass and flagrant violations of human rights and fundamental freedoms and those involving alien domination and foreign occupation, that may give rise to international terrorism and may endanger international peace and security;

7. Firmly calls for the immediate and safe release of all hostages and abducted persons, wherever and by whomever they are being held;

8. Calls upon all States to use their political influence in accordance with the Charter of the United Nations and the principles of international law to secure the safe release of all hostages and abducted persons and to prevent the commission of acts of hostage-taking and abduction;

9. Expresses concern at the growing and dangerous links between terrorist groups, drug traffickers and their paramilitary gangs, which have resorted to all types of violence, thus endangering the constitutional order of States and violating basic human rights;

10. Welcomes the efforts undertaken by the International Civil Aviation Organization aimed at promoting universal acceptance of, and strict compliance with, international air-security conventions, and welcomes its recent adoption of the Protocol for the Suppression of Unlawful Acts of Violence at Airports Serving International Civil Aviation;

11. Also welcomes the adoption by the International Maritime Organization of the Convention for the Suppression of Unlawful Acts against the Safety of Maritime Navigation and the Protocol for the Suppression of Unlawful Acts against the Safety of Fixed Platforms located on the Continental Shelf;

12. Urges the International Civil Aviation Organization to intensify its work on devising an international regime for the marking of plastic or sheet explosives for the purposes of detection;

13. Requests the other relevant specialized agencies and intergovernmental organizations, in particular the Universal Postal Union, the World Tourism Organization and the International Atomic Energy Agency, within their respective spheres of competence, to consider what further measures can usefully be taken to combat and eliminate terrorism;

14. Requests the Secretary-General to continue seeking the views of Member States on international terrorism in all its aspects and on ways and means of combating it, including the convening, under the auspices of the United Nations, of an

international conference to deal with international terrorism in the light of the proposal referred to in the penultimate preambular paragraph of the present resolution;

15. Also requests the Secretary-General to seek the views of Member States on the ways and means of enhancing the role of the United Nations and the relevant specialized agencies in combating international terrorism, as well as on proposals made during the debate on this item in the Sixth Committee at the forty-fourth session of the General Assembly;

16. Further requests the Secretary-General to follow up, as appropriate, the implementation of the present resolution and to submit a report in this respect to the General Assembly at its forty-sixth session;

17. Considers that nothing in the present resolution could in any way prejudice the right to self-determination, freedom and independence, as derived from the Charter of the United Nations, of peoples forcibly deprived of that right referred to in the Declaration on Principles of International Law concerning Friendly Relations and Co-operation among States in accordance with the Charter of the United Nations, particularly peoples under colonial and racist regimes or other forms of alien domination, or the right of these peoples to struggle legitimately to this end and to seek and receive support in accordance with the principles of the Charter, the above-mentioned Declaration and the relevant General Assembly resolutions, including the present resolution;

18. Decides to include the item in the provisional agenda of its forty-sixth session.

47

Note by the President of the Security Council (22 November 1989)

Following consultations with the members of the Security Council, the President of the Council made the following statement, on behalf of the Council, at its 2894th meeting, on 22 November 1989, in connection with the Council's consideration of the item entitled "The situation in the Middle East".

"The members of the Security Council express their deep indignation and dismay over the assassination of Mr. René Moawad, President of the Lebanese Republic, earlier today in Beirut. They express their sympathy and condolences to the family of the late President, to the Prime Minister and to the Lebanese people.

"The members of the Security Council strongly condemn this cowardly, criminal and terrorist act for what it is, an attack upon the unity of Lebanon, the democratic processes and the process of national reconciliation.

"The members of the Security Council recall their statement of 7 November 1989, and reaffirm their support for the efforts undertaken by the Tripartite High Committee of the League of Arab States and for the Taif agreement. These remain the only basis for guaranteeing the full sovereignty, independence, territorial integrity and national unity of Lebanon.

"The members of the Security Council reiterate their call of 7 November 1989 to all sectors of the Lebanese people to continue the process of achieving the goals of the restoration of the Lebanese State and the establishment of renovated institutions that had started with the election of President Moawad and the appointment of Prime Minister Selim El-Hoss. Democratic Lebanese institutions must be strongly supported and the process of national reconciliation must go forward. This is the only way that Lebanese national unity can be fully restored.

"The members of the Security Council solemnly reaffirm their support for the Taif agreement, ratified by the Lebanese Parliament on 5 November 1989. In this regard, they urge all Lebanese people to exercise restraint, to rededicate themselves to the urgent task of national reconciliation and to demonstrate their commitment to democratic processes.

"The members of the Security Council are convinced that all those who seek to divide the people of Lebanon through such cowardly, criminal and terrorist acts of violence cannot, and will not, succeed."

48

Convention for the Suppression of Unlawful Acts Against the Safety of Maritime Navigation (10 March 1988)

The States Parties to this Convention,

Having in Mind the purposes and principles of the Charter of the United Nations concerning the maintenance of international peace and security and the promotion of friendly relations and co-operation among States,

Recognizing in particular that everyone has the right to life, liberty and security of person, as set out in the Universal Declaration of Human Rights and the International Covenant on Civil and Political Rights,

Deeply Concerned about the world-wide escalation of acts of terrorism in all its forms, which endanger or take innocent human lives, jeopardize fundamental freedoms and seriously impair the dignity of human beings,

Considering that unlawful acts against the safety of maritime navigation jeopardize the safety of persons and property, seriously affect the operation of maritime services, and undermine the confidence of the peoples of the world in the safety of maritime navigation,

Considering that the occurrence of such acts is a matter of grave concern to the international community as a whole,

Being Convinced of the urgent need to develop international

co-operation between States in devising and adopting effective and practical measures for the prevention of all unlawful acts against the safety of maritime navigation, and the prosecution and punishment of their perpetrators,

Recalling resolution 40/61 of the General Assembly of the United Nations of 9 December 1985 which, inter alia, "urges all States unilaterally and in co-operation with other States, as well as relevant United Nations organs, to contribute to the progressive elimination of causes underlying international terrorism and to pay special attention to all situations, including colonialism, racism and situations involving mass and flagrant violations of human rights and fundamental freedoms and those involving alien occupation, that may give rise to international terrorism and may endanger international peace and security",

Recalling further that resolution 40/61 "unequivocally condemns, as criminal) all acts, methods and practices of terrorism wherever and by whomever committed, including those which jeopardize friendly relations among States and their security",

Recalling also that by resolution 40/61, the International Maritime Organization was invited to "study the problem of terrorism aboard or against ships with a view to making recommendations on appropriate measures",

Having in mind resolution A.584(14) of 20 November 1985, of the Assembly of the International Maritime Organization, which called for development of measures to prevent unlawful acts which threaten the safety of ships and the security of their passengers and crews,

Noting that acts of the crew which are subject to normal shipboard discipline are outside the purview of this Convention,

Affirming the desirability of monitoring rules and standards relating to the prevention and control of unlawful acts against ships and persons on board ships, with a view to updating them as necessary, and, to this effect, taking note with satisfaction of the Measures to Prevent Unlawful Acts against Passengers and Crews on Board Ships, recommended by the Maritime Safety Committee of the International Maritime Organization,

Affirming further that matters not regulated by this Convention continue to be governed by the rules and principles of general international law,

Recognizing the need for all States, in combating unlawful acts against the safety of maritime navigation, strictly to comply with rules and principles of general international law,

Have agreed as follows :

Article 1

For the purposes of this Convention, "ship" means a vessel of any type whatsoever not permanently attached to the sea-bed, including dynamically supported craft, submersibles, or any other floating craft.

Article 2

1. This Convention does not apply to :

(a) a warship; or

(b) a ship owned or operated by a State when being used as a naval auxiliary or for customs or police purposes; or

(c) a ship which has been withdrawn from navigation or laid up.

2. Nothing in this Convention affects the immunities of warships and other government ships operated for non-commercial purposes.

Article 3

1. Any person commits an offence if that person unlawfully and intentionally :

(a) seizes or exercises control over a ship by force or threat thereof or any other form of intimidation; or

(b) performs an act of violence against a person on board

a ship if that act is likely to endanger the safe navigation of that ship; or

(c) destroys a ship or causes damage to a ship or to its cargo which is likely to endanger the safe navigation of that ship; or

(d) places or causes to be placed on a ship, by any means whatsoever, a device or substance which is likely to destroy that ship, or cause damage to that ship or its cargo which endangers or is likely to endanger the safe navigation of that ship; or

(e) destroys or seriously damages maritime navigational facilities or seriously interferes with their operation, if any such act is likely to endanger the safe navigation of a ship; or

(f) communicates information which he knows to be false, thereby endangering the safe navigation of a ship; or

(g) injures or kills any person, in connection with the commission or the attempted commission of any of the offences set forth in subparagraphs (a) to (f).

2. Any person also commits an offence if that person :

(a) attempts to commit any of the offences set forth in paragraph 1; or

(b) abets the commission of any of the offences set forth in paragraph 1 perpetrated by any person or is otherwise an accomplice of a person who commits such an offence; or

(c) threatens, with or without a condition, as is provided for under national law, aimed at compelling a physical or juridical person to do or refrain from doing any act, to commit any of the of fences set forth in paragraph 1, subparagraphs (b), (c) and (e), if that threat is likely to endanger the safe navigation of the ship in question.

Article 4

1. This Convention applies if the ship is navigating of is scheduled to navigate into, through or from waters beyond the outer limit of the territorial sea of a single State, or the lateral limits of its territorial sea with adjacent States.

2. In cases where the Convention does not apply pursuant to paragraph 1, it nevertheless applies when the offender or the alleged offender is found in the territory of a State Party other than the State referred to in paragraph 1.

Article 5

Each State Party shall make the offences set forth in article 3 punishable by appropriate penalties which take into account the grave nature of those offences.

Article 6

1. Each State Party shall take such measures as may be necessary to establish its jurisdiction over the offences set forth in article 3 when the offence is committed :

(a) against or on board a ship flying the flag of the State at the time the offence is committed; or

(b) in the territory of that State, including its territorial sea; or

(c) by a national of that State.

2. A State Party may also establish its jurisdiction over any such offence when :

(a) it is committed by a stateless person whose habitual residence is in that State; or

(b) during its commission a national of that State is seized, threatened, injured or killed; or

(c) it is committed in an attempt to compel that State to do or abstain from doing any act.

3. Any State Party which has established jurisdiction mentioned in paragraph 2 shall notify the Secretary-General of the International Maritime Organization (hereinafter referred

to as "the Secretary-General"). If such State Party subsequently rescinds that jurisdiction, it shall notify the Secretary-General.

4. Each State Party shall take such measures as may be necessary to establish its jurisdiction over the offences set forth in article 3 in cases where the alleged offender is present in its territory and it does not extradite him to any of the States Parties which have established their jurisdiction in accordance with paragraphs 1 and 2 of this article.

5. This Convention does not exclude any criminal jurisdiction exercised in accordance with national law.

Article 7

1. Upon being satisfied that the circumstances so warrant, any State Party in the territory of which the offender or the alleged offender is present shall, in accordance with its law, take him into custody or take other measures to ensure his presence for such time as is necessary to enable any criminal or extradition proceedings to be instituted.

2. Such State shall immediately make a preliminary inquiry into the facts, in accordance with its own legislation.

3. Any person regarding whom the measures referred to in paragraph 1 are being taken shall be entitled to :

(a) communicate without delay with the nearest appropriate representative of the State of which he is a national or which is otherwise entitled to establish such communication or, if he is a stateless person, the State in the territory of which he has his habitual residence;

(b) be visited by a representative of that State.

4. The rights referred to in paragraph 3 shall be exercised in conformity with the laws and regulations of the State in the territory of which the offender or the alleged offender is present, subject to the proviso that the said laws and regulations must enable full effect to be given to the purposes for which the rights accorded under paragraph 3 are intended.

5. When a State Party, pursuant to this article, has taken a

person into custody, it shall immediately notify the States which have established jurisdiction in accordance with article 6, paragraph 1 and, if it considers it advisable, any other interested States, of the fact that such person is in custody and of the circumstances which warrant his detention. The State which makes the preliminary inquiry contemplated in paragraph 2 of this article shall promptly report its findings to the said States and shall indicate whether it intends to exercise jurisdiction.

Article 8

1. The master of a ship of a State Party (the "flag State") may deliver to the authorities of any other State Party (the "receiving State") any person who he has reasonable grounds to believe has committed one of the offences set forth in article 3.

2. The flag State shall ensure that the master of its ship is obliged, whenever practicable, and if possible before entering the territorial sea of the receiving State carrying on board any person whom the master intends to deliver in accordance with paragraph 1, to give notification to the authorities of the receiving State of his intention to deliver such person and the reasons therefor.

3. The receiving State shall accept the delivery, except where it has grounds to consider that the Convention is not applicable to the acts giving rise to the delivery, and shall proceed in accordance with the provisions of article 1. Any refusal to accept a delivery shall be accompanied by a statement of the reasons for refusal.

4. The flag State shall ensure that the master of its ship is obliged to furnish the authorities of the receiving State with the evidence in the master's possession which pertains to the alleged offence.

5. A receiving State which has accepted the delivery of a person in accordance with paragraph 3 may, in turn, request the flag State to accept delivery of that person. The flag State shall consider any such request, and if it accedes to the request

it shall proceed in accordance with article 7. If the flag State declines a request, it shall furnish the receiving State with a statement of the reasons therefor.

Article 9

Nothing in this Convention shall affect in any way the rules of international law pertaining to the competence of States to exercise investigative or enforcement jurisdiction on board ships not flying their flag.

Article 10

1. The State Party in the territory of which the offender or the alleged offender is found shall, in cases to which article 6 applies, if it does not extradite him, be obliged, without exception whatsoever and whether or not the offence was committed in its territory, to submit the case without delay to its competent authorities for the purpose of prosecution, through proceedings in accordance with the laws of that State. Those authorities shall take their decision in the same manner as in the case of any other offence of a grave nature under the law of that State.

2. Any person regarding whom proceedings are being carried out in connection with any of the offences set forth in article 3 shall be guaranteed fair treatment at all stages of the proceedings, including enjoyment of all the rights and guarantees provided for such proceedings by the law of the State in the territory of which he is present.

Article 11

1. The offences set forth in article 3 shall be deemed to be included as extraditable offences in any extradition treaty existing between any of the States Parties. States Parties undertake to include such offences as extraditable offences in every extradition treaty to be concluded between them.

2. If a State Party which makes extradition conditional on the existence of a treaty receives a request for extradition from another State Party with which it has no extradition treaty, the

requested State Party may, at its option, consider this Convention as a legal basis for extradition in respect of the offences set forth in article 3. Extradition shall be subject to the other conditions provided by the law of the requested State Party.

3. States Parties which do not make extradition conditional on the existence of a treaty shall recognize the offences set forth in article 3 as extraditable offences between themselves, subject to the conditions provided by the law of the requested State.

4. If necessary, the offences set forth in article 3 shall be treated, for the purposes of extradition between States Parties, as if they had been committed not only in the place in which they occurred but also in a place within the jurisdiction of the State Party requesting extradition.

5. A State Party which receives more than one request for extradition from States which have established jurisdiction in accordance with article 7 and which decides not to prosecute shall, in selecting the State to which the offender or alleged offender is to be extradited, pay due regard to the interests and responsibilities of the State Party whose flag the ship was flying at the time of the commission of the offence.

6. In considering a request for the extradition of an alleged offender pursuant to this Convention, the requested State shall pay due regard to whether his rights as set forth in article 7, paragraph 3, can be effected in the requesting State.

7. With respect to the offences as defined in this Convention, the provisions of all extradition treaties and arrangements applicable between States Parties are modified as between States Parties to the extent that they are incompatible with this Convention.

Article 12

1. State Parties shall afford one another the greatest measure of assistance in connection with criminal proceedings brought in respect of the offences set forth in article 3, including

assistance in obtaining evidence at their disposal necessary for the proceedings.

2. States Parties shall carry out their obligations under paragraph 1 in conformity with any treaties on mutual assistance that may exist between them. In the absence of such treaties, States Parties shall afford each other assistance in accordance with their national law.

Article 13

1. States Parties shall co-operate in the prevention of the offences set forth in article 3, particularly by :

(a) taking all practicable measures to prevent preparations in their respective territories for the commission of those offences within or outside their territories;

(b) exchanging information in accordance with their national law, and co-ordinating administrative and other measures taken as appropriate to prevent the commission of offences set forth in article 3.

2. When, due to the commission of an offence set forth in article 3, the passage of a ship has been delayed or interrupted, any State Party in whose territory the ship or passengers or crew are present shall be bound to exercise all possible efforts to avoid a ship, its passengers, crew or cargo being unduly detained or delayed.

Article 14

Any State Party having reason to believe that an offence set forth in article 3 will be committed shall, in accordance with its national law, furnish as promptly as possible any relevant information in its possession to those States which it believes would be the States having established jurisdiction in accordance with article 6.

Article 15

1. Each State Party shall, in accordance with its national law) provide to the Secretary-General, as promptly as possible, any relevant information in its possession concerning :

(a) the circumstances of the offence;

(b) the action taken pursuant to article 13, paragraph 2;

(c) the measures taken in relation to the offender or the alleged offender and, in particular, the results of any extradition proceedings or other legal proceedings.

2. The State Party where the alleged offender is prosecuted shall, in accordance with its national law, communicate the final outcome of the proceedings to the Secretary-General.

3. The information transmitted in accordance with paragraphs 1 and 2 shall be communicated by the Secretary-General to all States Parties, to Members of the International Maritime Organization (hereinafter referred to as "the Organization"), to the other States concerned, and to the appropriate international intergovernmental organizations.

Article 16

1. Any dispute between two or more States Parties concerning the interpretation or application of this Convention which cannot be settled through negotiation within a reasonable time shall, at the request of one of them, be submitted to arbitration. If, within six months from the date of the request for arbitration, the parties are unable to agree on the organization of the arbitration any one of those parties may refer the dispute to the International Court of Justice by request in conformity with the Statute of the Court.

2. Each State may at the time of signature or ratification, acceptance or approval of this Convention or accession thereto, declare that it does not consider itself bound by any or all of the provisions of paragraph 1. The other States Parties shall not be bound by those provisions with respect to any State Party which has made such a reservation.

3. Any State which has made a reservation in accordance with paragraph 2 may, at any time, withdraw that reservation by notification to the Secretary-General.

Article 17

1. This Convention shall be open for signature at Rome on 10 March 1988 by States participating in the International Conference on the Suppression of Unlawful Acts against the Safety of Maritime Navigation and at the Headquarters of the Organization by all States from 14 March 1988 to 9 March 1989. It shall thereafter remain open for accession.

2. States may express their consent to be bound by this Convention by :

(a) signature without reservation as to ratification, acceptance or approval; or

(b) signature subject to ratification, acceptance or approval, followed by ratification, acceptance or approval; or

(c) accession.

3. Ratification, acceptance, approval or accession shall be effected by the deposit of an instrument to that effect with the Secretary-General.

Article 18

1. This Convention shall enter into force ninety days following the date on which fifteen States have either signed it without reservation as to ratification, acceptance or approval, or have deposited an instrument of ratification, acceptance, approval or accession in respect thereof.

2. For a State which deposits an instrument of ratification, acceptance, approval or accession in respect of this Convention after the conditions for entry into force thereof have been met, the ratification, acceptance, approval or accession shall take effect ninety days after the date of such deposit.

Article 19

1. This Convention may be denounced by any State Party at any time after the expiry of one year from the date on which this Convention enters into force for that State.

2. Denunciation shall be effected by the deposit of an instrument of denunciation with the Secretary-General.

3. A denunciation shall take effect one year, or such longer period as may be specified in the instrument of denunciation, after the receipt of the instrument of denunciation by the Secretary-General.

Article 20

1. A conference for the purpose of revising or amending this Convention may be convened by the Organization.

2. The Secretary-General shall convene a conference of the States Parties to this Convention for revising or amending the Convention, at the request of one third of the States Parties, or ten States Parties, whichever is the higher figure.

3. Any instrument of ratification, acceptance, approval or accession deposited after the date of entry into force of an amendment to this Convention shall be deemed to apply to the Convention as amended.

Article 21

1. This Convention shall be deposited with the Secretary-General.

2. The Secretary-General shall :

(a) inform all States which have signed this Convention or acceded thereto, and all Members of the Organization, of :

(i) each new signature or deposit of an instrument of ratification, acceptance, approval or accession together with the date thereof;

(ii) the date of the entry into force of this Convention;

(iii) the deposit of any instrument of denunciation of this Convention together with the date on which it is received and the date on which the denunciation takes effect;

(iv) the receipt of any declaration or notification made under this Convention;

(b) transmit certified true copies of this Convention to all States which have signed this Convention or acceded thereto.

3. As soon as this Convention enters into force, a certified true copy thereof shall be transmitted by the Depositary to the Secretary-General of the United Nations for registration and publication in accordance with Article 102 of the Charter of the United Nations.

Article 22

This Convention is established in a single original in the Arabic, Chinese, English, French, Russian and Spanish languages, each text being equally authentic.

49

Protocol for the Suppression of Unlawful Acts Against the Safety of Fixed Platforms Located on the Continental Shelf (10 March 1988)

The States Parties to this Convention,

Being parties to the Convention for the Suppression of Unlawful Acts Against the Safety of Maritime Navigation,

Recognizing that the reasons for which the Convention was elaborated also apply to fixed platforms located on the continental shelf,

Taking account of the provisions of that Convention,

Affirming that matters not regulated by this Protocol continue to be governed by the rules and principles of general International law,

Hage agreed as follows :

Article 1

1. The provisions of articles 5 and 7 and of articles 10 to 16 of the Convention for the Suppression of unlawful Acts against the Safety of Maritime Navigation (hereafter referred to as "the Convention") shall also apply mutatis mutandis to the offences set forth in article 2 of this Protocol where such offences are committed on board or against fixed platforms located on the continental shelf.

2. In cases where this Protocol does not apply pursuant to paragraph 1, it nevertheless applies when the offender or the alleged offender is found in the territory of a State Party other than the State in whose international waters or territorial sea the fixed platform is located.

3. For the purposes of this Protocol, "fixed platform" means an artificial island, installation or structure permanently attached to the sea-bed for the purpose of exploration or exploitation of resources or for other economic purposes.

Article 2

1. Any person commits an offence if that person unlawfully and intentionally :

(a) seizes or exercises control over a fixed platform by force or threat thereof or any other form of intimidation; or

(b) performs an act of violence against a person on board a fixed platform if that act is likely to endanger its safety; or

(c) destroys a fixed platform or causes damage to it which is likely to endanger its safety; or

(d) places or causes to be placed on a fixed platform, by any means whatsoever, a device or substance which is likely to destroy that fixed platform or likely to endanger its safety; or

(e) injures or kills any person in connection with the commission or the attempted commission of any of the offences set forth in subparagraphs (a) to (d).

2. Any person also commits an offence if that person :

(a) attempts to commit any of the offences set forth in paragraph 1; or

(b) abets the commission of any such offences perpetrated by any person or is otherwise an accomplice of a person who commits such an offence; or

(c) threatens, with or without a condition, as is provided for under national law, aimed at compelling a physical or juridical person to do or refrain from doing any act, to commit any of the offences set forth in paragraph 1, subparagraphs (b) and (c), if that threat is likely to endanger the safety of the fixed platform.

Article 3

1. Each State Party shall take such measures as may be necessary to establish its jurisdiction over the offences set forth in article 2 when the offence is committed :

(a) against or on board a fixed platform while it is located on the continental shelf of that State; or

(b) by a national of that State.

2. A State Party may also establish its jurisdiction over any such offence when :

(a) it is committed by a stateless person whose habitual residence is in that State;

(b) during its commission a national of that State is seized, threatened, injured or killed; or

(c) it is committed in an attempt to compel that State to do or abstain from doing any act.

3. Any State Party which has established jurisdiction mentioned in paragraph 2 shall notify the Secretary-General of the International Maritime Organisation (hereinafter referred to as "the Secretary-General"). If such State Party subsequently rescinds that Jurisdiction, it shall notify the Secretary-General.

4. Each State Party shall take such measures as may be necessary to establish its jurisdiction over the offences set forth in article 2 in cases where the alleged offender is present in its territory and it does not extradite him to any of the States Parties which have established their jurisdiction in accordance with paragraphs 1 and 2 of this article.

5. This Protocol does not exclude any criminal jurisdiction exercised in accordance with national law.

Article 4

Nothing in this Protocol shall affect in any way the rules of international law pertaining to fixed platforms located on the continental shelf.

Article 5

1. This Protocol shall be open for signature at Rome on 10 March 1988 and at the Headquarters of the International Maritime Organization (hereinafter referred to as "the Organization") from 14 March 1988 to 9 March 1989 by any State which has signed the Convention. It shall thereafter remain open for accession.

2. States may express their consent to be bound by this Protocol by :

(a) signature without reservation as to ratification, acceptance or approval; or

(b) signature subject to ratification, acceptance or approval, followed by ratification, acceptance or approval; or

(c) accession.

3. Ratification, acceptance, approval or accession shall be effected by the deposit of an instrument to that effect with the Secretary-General.

4. Only a State which has signed the Convention without reservation as to ratification, acceptance or approval, or has ratified, accepted, approved or acceded to the Convention may become a Party to this Protocol.

Article 6

1. This Protocol shall enter into force ninety days following the date on which three States have either signed it without reservation as to ratification, acceptance or approval, or have deposited an instrument of ratification, acceptance, approval or accession in respect thereof. However, this Protocol shall not enter into force before the Convention has entered into force.

2. For a State which deposits an instrument of ratification,

acceptance, approval or accession in respect of this Protocol after the conditions for entry into force thereof have been met, the ratification, acceptance, approval or accession shall take effect ninety days after the date of such deposit.

Article 7

1. This Protocol may be denounced by any State Party at any time after the expiry of one year from the date on which this Protocol enters into force for that State.

2. Denunciation shall be effected by the deposit of an instrument of denunciation with the Secretary-General.

3. A denunciation shall take effect one year, or such longer period as may be specified in the instrument of denunciation, after the receipt of the instrument of denunciation by the Secretary-General.

4. A denunciation of the Convention by a State Party shall be deemed to be a denunciation of this Protocol by that Party.

Article 8

1. A conference for the purpose of revising or amending this Protocol may be convened by the Organization.

2. The Secretary-General shall convene a conference of the States Parties to this Protocol for revising or amending the Protocol, at the request of one third of the States Parties, or five States Parties, whichever is the higher figure.

3. Any instrument of ratification, acceptance, approval or accession deposited after the date of entry into force of an amendment to this Protocol shall be deemed to apply to the Protocol as amended.

Article 9

1. This Protocol shall be deposited with the Secretary-General.

2. The Secretary-General shall :

(a) inform all States which have signed this Protocol or

acceded thereto, and all Members of the Organization, of :

(i) each new signature or deposit of an instrument of ratification, acceptance, approval or accession, together with the date thereof;

(ii) the date of entry into force of this Protocol;

(iii) the deposit of any instrument of denunciation of this Protocol together with the date on which it is received and the date on which the denunciation takes effect;

(iv) the receipt of any declaration or notification made under this Protocol or under the Convention, concerning this Protocol.

(b) transmit certified true copies of this Protocol to all States which have signed this Protocol or acceded thereto

3. As soon as this Protocol enters into force, a certified true copy thereof shall be transmitted by the Depositary to the Secretary-General of the United Nations for registration and publication in accordance with Article 102 of the Charter of the United Nations.

Article 10

1. This Protocol is established in a single original in the Arabic, Chinese, English, French, Russian and Spanish languages, each text being equally authentic.

50

Measures to Prevent International Terrorism (42/159, 7 December 1987)

Measures to prevent international terrorism which endangers or takes innocent human lives or jeopardizes fundamental freedoms and study of the underlying causes of those forms of terrorism and acts of violence which lie in misery, frustration, grievance and despair and which cause some people to sacrifice human lives, including their own, in an attempt to effect radical changes :

(a) Report of the Secretary-General;

(b) Convening, under the auspices of the United Nations, of an international conference to define terrorism and to differentiate it from the struggle of peoples for national liberation

The General Assembly,

Recalling its resolutions 3034 (XXVII) of 18 December 1972, 31/102 of 15 December 1976, 32/147 of 16 December 1977, 34/145 of 17 December 1979, 36/109 of 10 December 1981 and 38/130 of 19 December 1983,

Reaffirming its resolution 40/61 of 9 December 1985, adopted without a vote, and the importance thereof in the consideration of the question of international terrorism and, in particular, in the strengthening of co-operation in preventing and eliminating terrorism,

Recalling the recommendations of the Ad Hoc Committee on International Terrorism contained in its report to the General Assembly at its thirty-fourth session,

Recalling also the Declaration on Principles of International Law concerning Friendly Relations and Co-operation among States in accordance with the Charter of the United Nations, the Declaration on the Strengthening of International Security, the Definition of Aggression and relevant instruments on international humanitarian law applicable in armed conflict,

Further recalling the existing international conventions relating to various aspects of the problem of international terrorism, inter alia, the Convention on Offences and Certain Other Acts Committed on Board Aircraft, signed at Tokyo on 14 September 1963, the Convention for the Suppression of Unlawful Seizure of Aircraft, signed at The Hague on 16 December 1970, the Convention for the Suppression of Unlawful Acts against the Safety of Civil Aviation, concluded at Montreal on 23 September 1971, the Convention on the Prevention and Punishment of Crimes against Internationally Protected Persons, including Diplomatic Agents, adopted at New York on 14 December 1973, and the International Convention against the Taking of Hostages, adopted at New York on 17 December 1979, as well as the Convention on the Physical Protection of Nuclear Material, adopted at Vienna on 3 March 1980,

Convinced of the importance of the observance by States of their obligations under the relevant international conventions to ensure that appropriate law enforcement measures are taken in connection with the offences addressed in those conventions,

Deploring the continuation of all terrorist acts, including those in which States are directly or indirectly involved, which spread violence and terror, may result in loss of human lives and material damage and jeopardize the normal functioning of international relations,

Deeply disturbed by the world-wide persistence of those acts of international terrorism which can pose a threat to international peace and security and to friendly relations among States,

Convinced of the importance of expanding and improving international co-operation among States, on a bilateral, regional and multilateral basis, which will contribute to the elimination of acts of international terrorism and their underlying causes and to the prevention and elimination of this criminal scourge,

Convinced that international co-operation in combating and preventing terrorism will contribute to the strengthening of confidence among States, reduce tensions and create a better climate among them,

Reaffirming the principle of the self-determination of peoples as enshrined in the Charter of the United Nations,

Reaffirming also the inalienable right to self-determination and independence of all peoples under colonial and racist regimes and other forms of alien domination, and upholding the legitimacy of their struggle, in particular the struggle of national liberation movements, in accordance with the purposes and principles of the Charter and of the Declaration on Principles of International Law concerning Friendly Relations and Co-operation among States in accordance with the Charter of the United Nations,

Noting the efforts and important achievements of the International Civil Aviation Organization and the International Maritime Organization in promoting the security of international air and sea transport against acts of terrorism, consistent with General Assembly resolution 40/61,

Appealing to all States to take all appropriate steps to prevent terrorist attacks against various forms of public transport,

Urging all States to take effective measures, in accordance with established principles of international law, in order that all acts, methods and practices of international terrorism may be brought to an end,

Mindful of the necessity of maintaining and safeguarding the basic rights of the individual in accordance with the relevant international human rights instruments and generally accepted international standards,

Recognizing that the effectiveness of the struggle against terrorism could be enhanced by the establishment of a generally agreed definition of international terrorism,

Taking into account the proposal made at its forty-second session to hold an international conference on international terrorism, as referred to in agenda item 126 (b),

Taking note of the report of the Secretary-General,

1. Once again unequivocally condemns, as criminal, all acts, methods and practices of terrorism wherever and by whomever committed, including those which jeopardize friendly relations among States and their security;

2. Deeply deplores the loss of human lives which results from such acts of terrorism;

3. Also deplores the pernicious impact of acts of international terrorism on relations of co-operation among States, including co-operation for development;

4. Calls upon all States to fulfil their obligations under international law to refrain from organizing, instigating, assisting or participating in terrorist acts in other States, or acquiescing in activities within their territory directed towards the commission of such acts;

5. Urges all States to fulfil their obligations under international law and to take effective and resolute measures for the speedy and final elimination of international terrorism and, to that end :

(a) To prevent the preparation and organization in their respective territories, for commission within or outside their territories, of terrorist acts and subversive acts directed against other States and their citizens;

(b) To ensure the apprehension and prosecution or extradition of perpetrators of terrorist acts;

(c) To endeavour to conclude special agreements to that effect on a bilateral, regional and multilateral basis;

(d) To co-operate with one another in exchanging relevant information concerning the prevention and combating of terrorism;

(e) To harmonize their domestic legislation with the existing international conventions on this subject to which they are parties;

6. Appeals to all States that have not yet done so to consider becoming party to the international conventions relating to various aspects of international terrorism referred to in the preamble to the present resolution;

7. Urges all States not to allow any circumstances to obstruct the application of appropriate law enforcement measures provided for in the relevant conventions to which they are party to persons who commit acts of international terrorism covered by those conventions;

8. Also urges all States, unilaterally and in co-operation with other States, as well as relevant United Nations organs, to contribute to the progressive elimination of the causes underlying international terrorism and to pay special attention to all situations, including colonialism, racism and situations involving mass and flagrant violations of human rights and fundamental freedoms and those involving alien domination and occupation, that may give rise to international terrorism and may endanger international peace and security;

9. Welcomes the efforts undertaken by the International Civil Aviation Organization aimed at promoting universal acceptance of and strict compliance with international air-security conventions, and its ongoing work on a new instrument

for the suppression of unlawful acts of violence at airports serving international civil aviation;

10. Also welcomes the work undertaken by the International Maritime Organization on the problem of terrorism on board or against ships, and the initiative under way to draft instruments on the suppression of unlawful acts against the safety of maritime navigation and of fixed platforms on the continental shelf;

11. Requests the other relevant specialized agencies and intergovernmental organizations, in particular the Universal Postal Union, the World Tourism Organization and the International Atomic Energy Agency, within their respective spheres of competence, to consider what further measures can usefully be taken to combat and eliminate terrorism;

12. Requests the Secretary-General to seek the views of Member States on international terrorism in all its aspects and on ways and means of combating it, including, inter alia, the convening, under the auspices of the United Nations, of an international conference to deal with international terrorism in the light of the proposal referred to in the penultimate preambular paragraph of the present resolution;

13. Further requests the Secretary-General to follow up, as appropriate, the implementation of the present resolution and to submit a report in this respect to the General Assembly at its forty-fourth session;

14. Considers that nothing in the present resolution could in any way prejudice the right to self-determination, freedom and independence, as derived from the Charter of the United Nations, of peoples forcibly deprived of that right referred to in the Declaration on Principles of International Law concerning Friendly Relations and Co-operation among States in accordance with the Charter of the United Nations, particularly peoples under colonial and racist regimes and foreign occupation or

other forms of colonial domination, nor, in accordance with the principles of the Charter and in conformity with the above-mentioned Declaration, the right of these peoples to struggle to this end and to seek and receive support;

15. Decides to include the item in the provisional agenda of its forty-fourth session.